INTRODUCTION TO ECONOMICS

Workbook

INTRODUCTION TO ECONOMICS

Workbook

Hannah Kling, PhD

TAN Books
Gastonia, North Carolina

Compiled by Hannah Kling, PhD

Cover design by Caroline Green

Cover image: *Jesus and the Tribute Money* by duncan1890/iStock

ISBN: 978-1-5051-2186-5

Published in the United States by
TAN Books
PO Box 269
Gastonia, NC 28053
www.TANBooks.com

Printed in the United States of America

Contents

How to Approach This Course

1. Do the vocabulary matching activity. This is open book, so use the glossary at the back of the book, as well as a dictionary or internet search, to identify the correct answers. Some vocabulary may include review terms from previous sections.
2. Read the associated section or sections of the book and watch the lecture. Take notes on both. Look up any terms you don't know.
3. Take the quiz without referring to your notes or the book. Check your answers; if you got fewer than eight correct, review the book, lecture, and your notes, and try again.
4. Write answers to the short answer questions. You can use your notes, the book, and the lecture to help you. Compare what you wrote to the suggested answers and guidelines to make sure you have understood the material. If possible, discuss your answers with someone else.
5. Optional: Look at any supplemental material listed.

Course Outline

Module	Lecture #	Topic	Book section
Module 1	**1**	**Introduction**	**1**
1	2	Incentives Matter	1.1
1	3	Opportunity Cost	1.2
1	4	Thinking on the Margins	1.3
1	5	Trade and Comparative Advantage	1.4
1	6	Transaction Costs	1.5
1	7	Demand and Supply	1.6
1	8	Prices and Equilibrium	1.6
1	9	Profit and Loss	1.7
1	10	Income and Value	1.8
1	11	Invisible Hand	1.11
1	12	Unintended Consequences	1.12
Module 2	**13**	**Introduction to Living Standards**	**1.9**
2	14	Sources of Economic Progress	1.10
2	15	Legal System	2.1
2	16	Competitive Markets	2.2
2	17	Limits on Regulation	2.3
2	18	Efficient Capital Market	2.4
2	19	Monetary Stability	2.5
2	20	Low Tax Rates	2.6
2	21	Free Trade	2.7
Module 3	**22**	**Introduction to Public Choice**	**3**
3	23	Market Inefficiencies	3.1-3.3
3	24	Political Decision-Making	3.4-3.8
3	25	Economic Systems	3.9-3.10
Module 4	**26**	**Introduction to Personal Finance**	**4**
4	27	Earnings	4.1-4.2
4	28	Budgeting	4.3-4.6
4	29	Compounding Growth	4.7
4	30	Investing	4.8-4.10
4	31	Managing Risk	4.11-4.12
	32	Conclusion	

Lecture 1

INTRODUCTION

Vocabulary

(Open book: Students should use the glossary at the back of the book, as well as a dictionary, to identify the correct answers. Format: matching)

Incentives	An input used to produce economic goods and services. Natural resources, labor, skills, entrepreneurial talent, and capital are examples.
Scarcity	The expected payoffs from actions
Resource	Distribute for a particular purpose
Allocate	Condition in which people would like to have more of a good or resources than is freely available from na-ture

Quiz

(Closed book)

1. MC: Economics is all about:
   A. banking.
   B. politics.
   C. human choices.

2. T/F: An economic system is a set of rules about how scarce goods and resources are allocated in a society.

3. MC: Why must we make choices?
   A. Because of scarcity.
   B. Because we have too many options.
   C. Because of poverty.

4. T/F: Prices are the only way to allocate goods and services.

5. MC: What causes competition?
    A. capitalism
    B. scarcity
    C. selfishness

6. MC: Economic thinking can help us:
    A. decide which goals to pursue.
    B. know which goals are most important.
    C. figure out how best to pursue our goals.

7. MC: What is the building-block economic action?
    A. trade
    B. investing in stocks and bonds
    C. building factories

8. MC: Which of the following are resources?
    A. coordination, scarcity, and allocation
    B. land, labor, and time
    C. neither A or B

9. T/F: Economics can help us understand why some countries grow and prosper and others remain poor.

10. MC: The richest people:
    A. have finite, limited resources.
    B. have unlimited resources.
    C. don't need to make tradeoffs.

Short Answer

1. What are some ways to allocate goods? Which do you think would be most fair, and why?

2. How are scarcity, tradeoffs, and choice related?

Optional Watching

"The Surprising Truth About What Motivates Us | Dan Pink," TheNuvoEntrepreneur, https://www.youtube.com/watch?v=KgGhSOAtAyQ

Lecture 2

Incentives Matter

Vocabulary

(Open book: Students should use the glossary at the back of the book, as well as a dictionary, to identify the correct answers. Format: matching)

Incentives	A hypothesis advanced as an essential presupposition, condition, or premise of a train of reasoning
Monetary	Not in the form of money
Non-monetary	An abstract concept that encompasses the trading arrangements of buyers and sellers that underlie the forces of supply and demand
Capitalism	Having or showing an unselfish concern for the welfare of others
Socialism	An economic system characterized by private or corporate ownership of capital goods, by investments that are determined by private decision, and by prices, production, and the distribution of goods that are determined mainly by competition in a free market
Input	The expected payoffs from actions
Altruistic	Overly concerned or preoccupied with material possessions rather than with intellectual or spiritual things
Postulate	An economic system characterized by collective or governmental ownership and administration of the means of production and distribution of goods
Materialistic	Relating to money
Market	A component of production (such as land, labor, or raw materials)

Quiz

(Closed book)

1. MC: Incentives are:
   - A. anything that motivates people.
   - B. the unexpected results of a choice.
   - C. always positive.

2. MC: Incentives matter because:
   - A. people care only about themselves.
   - B. people care mainly about money.
   - C. people weigh the costs and benefits of any choice.

3. T/F: Incentives only matter under capitalism; they are irrelevant in a socialist economy.

4. MC: If people want to buy more of an item than sellers are offering at the current price:
   - A. the price of the item will fall.
   - B. the price of the item will rise.
   - C. there will be excess supply of the item.

5. MC: Changes in market prices:
   - A. do not affect sellers' or buyers' incentives.
   - B. often cause permanent shortages of things people need.
   - C. change incentives in a way that brings the amount demanded and the amount supplied into balance.

6. T/F: People respond to incentives in a predictable way.

7. MC: When prices go up:
   - A. consumers' costs go up.
   - B. sellers' benefits go up.
   - C. both A and B.

8. MC: If sellers cannot sell all their goods at the current price, they will have to cut the price. How will the new, lower price affect buyers and sellers?
   - A. Buyers will want to purchase more, and sellers will want to produce more.
   - B. Buyers will want to purchase more, and sellers will want to produce less.
   - C. Buyers will want to buy less, and sellers will want to produce less.

9. MC: What caused glass factories in the Soviet Union to stop producing thick glass and start producing thin glass?
   - A. Their incentives changed.
   - B. Consumers demanded thinner glass.
   - C. The market price of glass changed.

10. T/F: Mother Teresa was self-interested.

Short Answer

1. Why would a person be more likely to bend down to pick up a quarter than a penny?
2. Suppose you can spend your summer enjoying the beach or taking a job at the local fast-food restaurant. What change in incentives would make it more likely for you to take the job? What would make it less likely?
3. What is the difference between being self-interested and being selfish?
4. Besides money, what other kinds of costs and benefits do people think about when making choices?

4. T/F: Costs are always measured in money.

5. MC: We live in a world of scarcity because:
   A. the productive resources on earth are limited and our needs and wants are unlimited.
   B. some people have more than their fair share of resources.
   C. we fail to consider opportunity costs.

6. MC: Scarcity forces us to make:
   A. bad choices.
   B. tradeoffs.
   C. money.

7. MC: Government cannot make things free, it can only:
   A. eliminate opportunity costs.
   B. shift costs.
   C. guide resources to their highest valued use.

8. MC: High costs for resources signal to producers that:
   A. those resources have other highly valued uses.
   B. consumers are willing to pay more for their product.
   C. owners of those resources are greedy.

9. MC: Opportunity cost is:
   A. an abstract idea that does not apply to people's actual behavior.
   B. how much money something costs.
   C. the value of the next-best alternative.

10. MC: If education is so important, why don't we spend a lot more on it?
   A. Because doing so involves tradeoffs with other important goals.
   B. Because many people underestimate the value of education.
   C. Because the opportunity cost of doing so is too low.

Short Answer

1. What is the difference between scarcity and poverty?

2. Why does scarcity always exist?

3. Why is there "no such thing as a free lunch," even if you don't have to pay any money for it?

4. What is *your* opportunity cost of spending $40 on a new shirt?

Lecture 4

THINKING ON THE MARGINS

Vocabulary

(Open book: Students should use the glossary at the back of the book, as well as a dictionary, to identify the correct answers. Format: matching)

Marginal	The change in total cost resulting from an action such as the production of an additional unit of output
Marginal benefit	Decreasing, declining
Marginal cost	A term used to describe the effects of a change in the current situation; additional
Diminishing	Benefit or value
Utility	The change in total value or benefit derived from an action such as consumption of an additional unit of a good or service

Quiz

(Closed book)

1. MC: When deciding, we look at the ____________ benefits and costs of that choice.
   A. average
   B. total
   C. marginal

2. MC: Which of the following is an example of making a choice on the margin?
   A. Choosing between having food and having clothing.
   B. Choosing between spending their next dollar on additional food or additional clothing.
   C. Equalizing the average value of food and clothing consumed.

3. MC: As people consume more food, the marginal benefit of more food:
   A. increases.
   B. decreases.
   C. stays the same.

4. MC: From an economic point of view, if we currently spend $1 million reducing pollution, should we spend more or less?
   A. Spend less because pollution reduction is a non-economic good.
   B. There's not enough information to say. We need to know the marginal costs and benefits of additional spending.
   C. There's not enough information to say. We need to know how much pollution costs us.

5. MC: As you have more of one thing, additional units tend to:
   A. be more and more valuable.
   B. be less and less valuable.
   C. stay the same value.

6. T/F: To make the most of our resources, we should take any actions where the benefits outweigh the costs, and none where the costs outweigh the benefits.

7. MC: People usually:
   A. pay attention to marginal analysis in their personal actions and their votes.
   B. pay attention to marginal analysis when voting, but often do not in their personal actions.
   C. pay attention to marginal analysis when making personal choices, but often not when voting.

8. MC: Under the equimarginal principal, you should:
   A. spend more of your money on things that are most important.
   B. spend your money so that the marginal value of the most important things is highest.
   C. spend your money so that the marginal value per dollar of all your purchases is equal.

9. MC: The more you have of something, the less valuable one additional unit tends to be. This is what economists call:
   A. the law of diminishing marginal utility.
   B. the law of supply and demand.
   C. the rule of law.

10. T/F: The marginal cost of a choice is the same as an average cost.

Short Answer

1. Suppose you are buying milk. You can buy a gallon for $3 or a half-gallon for $2. Which is the cheapest per gallon? Which should you buy? Why?
2. What is a choice you have made recently? Explain the choice using marginal analysis.
3. Is the marginal utility of a particular good fixed or variable? Why?

Lecture 5

Trade and Comparative Advantage

Vocabulary

(Open book: Students should use the glossary at the back of the book, as well as a dictionary, to identify the correct answers. Format: matching)

Value	Reductions in the firm's per-unit costs that occur when large factories are used to produce large volumes of output
Allocate	A method that breaks down the production of a commodity into a series of specific tasks, each per-formed by a different worker
Division of labor	Individuals, firms, regions or nations can produce a larger output and achieve mutual gains from trade by specializing in the production of goods they can produce at low opportunity cost
Specialization	The importance, worth, or usefulness of something
Economies of scale	Distribute for a particular purpose
Law of comparative advantage	The process of concentrating on and becoming expert in a particular subject or skill

Quiz

(Closed book)

1. MC: The wealth of a nation is determined by:
    A. the number of jobs that are created.
    B. how much money is in circulation.
    C. its production of goods and services, and their allocation.

2. MC: The law of comparative advantage says you should:
    A. produce what you produce best, and trade for the rest.
    B. produce as much as you can for yourself.
    C. produce the things for which you are a high-cost producer.

3. MC: Specialization means:
    A. goods move from people who value them less to people who value them more.
    B. individuals can focus on what they are better at producing.
    C. trade is zero-sum.

4. T/F: Trade can only increase the value of goods when something new is produced.

5. MC: Companies can take advantage of economies of scale only when:
    A. they have a broad market in which to sell.
    B. they are in a seller's market.
    C. they have a dominant market share.

For questions 6-8, suppose that in one day Tom can weave 6 baskets or pick 2 flats of strawberries. Mary can weave 2 baskets or pick 4 flats of strawberries in a day.

6. MC: What is Tom's opportunity cost of picking one flat of strawberries?
    A. 2 baskets
    B. 3 baskets
    C. 6 baskets

7. MC: What is Mary's opportunity cost of picking one flat of strawberries?
    A. ½ basket
    B. 2 baskets
    C. 4 baskets

8. MC: Who has the comparative advantage in strawberry picking?
    A. Mary: her opportunity cost of doing so is lower.
    B. Tom: his opportunity cost of doing so is higher.
    C. Neither: their opportunity costs are the same.

9. MC: What is a positive-sum activity?
    A. one in which one person's gain is another person's loss
    B. one in which two people gain at the expense of a third person
    C. one in which both people gain

10. MC: According to Adam Smith, the propensity to trade is:
    A. unique to Western Civilization.
    B. common to all humans.
    C. common to all higher mammals.

Short Answer

1. How does the idea of opportunity cost relate to comparative advantage?
2. What do economists mean when they say value is subjective? Come up with examples not used in the book or lecture.
3. List three reasons trade is beneficial.

Suggested Reading

"I, Pencil," by Leonard Read

Lecture 6

Transaction Costs

Vocabulary

(Open book: Students should use the glossary at the back of the book, as well as a dictionary, to identify the correct answers. Format: matching)

Transaction costs	The maximum amount a country can produce given its inputs
Productive capacity	A requirement that a person obtain permission from the government in order to perform certain business activities or work in certain occupations
Tariff	People who buy and sell goods or services or arrange trades
Quota	The time, effort, and other resources needed to search out, negotiate, and consummate an exchange of goods or services
Occupational licensing	A tax on imports
Price controls	A specific limit or maximum quantity or value of a good that is permitted to be imported into a country during a given period
Middlemen	Prices that are imposed by the government. The prices may be set either above or below the level that would be established by markets.

Lecture 3

Opportunity Cost

Vocabulary

(Open book: Students should use the glossary at the back of the book, as well as a dictionary, to identify the correct answers. Format: matching)

Resource	A government payment or tax credit provided to either the producers or consumers of certain goods
Scarcity	An input used to produce economic goods and services. Natural resources, labor, skills, entrepreneurial talent, and capital are examples
Opportunity cost	Condition in which people would like to have more of a good or resources than is freely available from nature
Forgo	Omit or decline to take (something pleasant or valuable); go without
Subsidy	The highest valued alternative good or activity that must be sacrificed as a result of choosing an option

Quiz

(Closed book)

1. T/F: Good choices don't have costs.

2. MC: In order to get something, we must give up something else that we:
    A. don't need.
    B. deserve.
    C. value.

3. T/F: Some things are too important to consider the costs involved.

Quiz

(Closed book)

1. MC: Factors that make it more difficult to trade are called:
    A. transaction costs.
    B. middlemen.
    C. involuntary costs.

2. MC: A middleman:
    A. provides value by improving the quality of a product.
    B. provides value by reducing transaction costs.
    C. reduces value by increasing the cost of goods.

3. MC: Changes that reduce transaction costs will:
    A. increase trade.
    B. limit economic growth.
    C. cause socialism.

4. MC: Price controls are an example of:
    A. political obstacles.
    B. search costs.
    C. reductions in transaction costs.

5. T/F: The market arranges trades automatically; they require no time or effort.

6. MC: Which of the following is not a source of transaction costs?
    A. bandits
    B. wear and tear on a car from commuting to work
    C. the labor that goes into building a house

7. MC: What has significantly reduced transaction costs in recent years?
    A. barter
    B. technology
    C. gains from trade

8. MC: Which of the following is not steadily decreasing due to innovation?
    A. transportation costs
    B. search costs
    C. political obstacles

9. T/F: Transaction costs are always included in the purchase price of a product.

10. T/F: Transaction costs reduce economic growth.

Short Answer

1. Give three examples not mentioned in the book or lecture of professions or innovations that reduce transaction costs.
2. How does putting a brand (e.g., McDonald's or Nike) on a product reduce transaction costs? What kind of transaction costs does this reduce?
3. Thinking back to what you have learned in the last two sections, why are geographic barriers to trade costly? Why couldn't we do just as well trading with people who are nearby rather than far away?

Lecture 7

Demand and Supply

Vocabulary

(Open book: Students should use the glossary at the back of the book, as well as a dictionary, to identify the correct answers. Format: matching)

Law of demand	The amount people want to buy at a particular price. (A single point on the demand curve.)
Demand	The quantity people are willing to supply at any given price. (Represented by an upward-sloping curve.)
Quantity demanded	The opportunity cost of the inputs
Law of supply	The quantity people want to buy at any given price. (Represented by a downward-sloping curve.)
Supply	As the price of something rises, producers are willing to supply more. As the price falls, producers supply less.
Quantity supplied	As the price of something rises, people want to buy less of it. As the price falls, people want to buy more.
Cost of production	The amount that will be supplied at a particular price. (A single point on the supply curve.)

Quiz

(Closed book)

1. MC: Demand slopes down because of:
    A. transaction costs.
    B. diminishing marginal utility.
    C. the allocation of resources.

2. MC: A demand graph shows:
    A. price per unit on the vertical axis, quantity sold on the horizontal axis.
    B. total spending on the vertical axis, quantity sold on the horizontal axis.
    C. demand on the horizontal axis, supply on the vertical axis.

3. MC: A demand curve:
    A. is a smooth, downward-sloping curve.
    B. must slope downward in a straight line.
    C. slopes downward, need not be a smooth curve or straight line.

4. MC: The opportunity cost of inputs:
    A. decreases as more of a good is produced.
    B. increases as more of a good is produced.
    C. stays constant no matter how much is produced.

5. T/F: The supply curve slopes downward because of diminishing marginal utility.

6. MC: A supply curve shows:
    A. quantity supplied on the vertical axis, quantity demanded on the horizontal axis.
    B. quantity supplied on the horizontal axis, price per unit on the vertical axis.
    C. subjective value on the vertical axis, marginal utility on the horizontal axis.

7. MC: Based on the law of supply:
    A. it takes higher wages to get you to work more hours.
    B. it takes lower wages to get you to work more hours.
    C. people will work the same number of hours regardless of their wages.

8. MC: Suppliers will only produce if the price they receive is greater than:
    A. the transaction costs.
    B. the demand.
    C. their costs.

9. MC: Cost of production is the opportunity cost of the:
    A. inputs.
    B. product.
    C. quantity demanded.

10. T/F: The height of the demand curve at any quantity shows the marginal utility of that unit.

Short Answer

1. Draw the graph of demand for tickets to a theme park using the following data:

Price	Quantity
$30	3,000
$25	4,000
$20	5,000
$15	6,000

2. Use the data above to answer: In what price range would you estimate people would buy 4,500 tickets?

3. Provide a graph of the supply of scarves.

Price	Quantity
$25	500
$20	350
$15	200
$10	50

4. Use the data above to answer:

   A. At what price will the seller be willing to produce 200 scarves?
   B. Estimate the quantity of scarves the seller would produce at a price of $22.

5. What do demand and supply curves represent?

6. What general rule applies to the shape of demand curves? Why is this? Why can the shape nevertheless vary?

Lecture 8

Prices and Equilibrium

Vocabulary

(Open book: Students should use the glossary at the back of the book, as well as a dictionary, to identify the correct answers. Format: matching)

Equilibrium	Products that serve similar purposes
Economic efficiency	A condition in which the amount of a good offered for sale by producers is greater than the amount that buyers will purchase at the existing price
Substitute goods	The price that brings supply and demand into balance
Shortage	A condition in which all actions for which the benefits exceed the cost are taken, and no actions for which the cost exceeds the benefits are taken
Surplus	A condition in which the amount of a good offered for sale by producers is less than the amount demanded by buyers at the existing price

Quiz

(Closed book)

1. T/F: Not every good and service has an equilibrium market price.

2. MC: At the equilibrium price:
   A. what each person pays matches the marginal utility to himself or herself.
   B. some consumers pay less than their marginal utility, and no consumers pay more.
   C. some consumers pay more than their marginal utility, and none pay less.

3. The price will tend to move:
   A. toward the quantity demanded.

B. away from the equilibrium price.
C. toward the equilibrium price.

4. MC: An increase in the price of one product:
   A. causes an increase in the demand for substitutes.
   B. causes a decrease in the demand for substitutes.
   C. causes a decrease in the price of substitutes.

5. T/F: If sellers find themselves with excess inventories, some will lower the price to sell this excess.

6. MC: Hayek believed the price system was:
   A. one of the greatest triumphs of the human mind.
   B. not the result of deliberate human design.
   C. something that was created by the auction system on eBay.

7. MC: Changes in price influence:
   A. quantity demanded.
   B. demand.
   C. equilibrium.

8. MC: A decrease in the supply of a good or service means:
   A. sellers are now willing to sell fewer units at any given price.
   B. buyers are now willing to buy fewer units at any given price.
   C. there will be a permanent shortage.

9. Market adjustments take place:
   A. instantaneously.
   B. only when producers and consumers learn about all the factors affecting supply and demand.
   C. only when consumers and producers adjust their actions to changes in supply or demand.

10. MC: Market prices:
   A. bring the quantity supplied and quantity demanded into balance.
   B. direct producers to supply those goods that consumers value more than their cost of production.
   C. both A and B.

Short Answer

1. At the equilibrium price, every buyer willing to pay the price is able to do so, and every seller willing to accept the price is able to do so. Why isn't this true at other prices?
2. Why do prices tend to move toward equilibrium in a market system?
3. What is the difference between demand and quantity demanded?
4. What are some factors that could cause a shift in demand?
5. Why would a price change in the market for one good affect prices in other markets?

Lecture 9

Profit and Loss

Vocabulary

(Open book: Students should use the glossary at the back of the book, as well as a dictionary, to identify the correct answers. Format: matching)

Profit	Price of all goods sold times quantity of goods sold
Cost	Buildings, tools, machinery, and other equipment used in production
Loss	Someone who takes risks and brings new products or services to the market
Entrepreneur	The amount by which sales revenue fails to cover the cost of supplying a good or service
Capital	The opportunity cost of inputs
Revenue	The amount by which total revenue exceeds total cost

Quiz

(Closed book)

1. MC: Businesses acquire resources by bidding them away from:
    A. alternative uses.
    B. consumers.
    C. laborers.

2. T/F: Another term for inputs is productive resources.

3. MC: Opportunity cost, unlike accounting cost, accounts for:
    A. alternative uses of assets owned by the firm.
    B. alternative uses of inputs bought by the firm.
    C. all possible alternative uses, not just the highest-valued alternative uses.

4. MC: Economic profit is:
    A. revenue minus accounting costs.
    B. revenue minus opportunity costs.
    C. opportunity costs minus accounting costs.

5. MC: A business makes an economic profit if:
    A. consumers value its product more than any other products.
    B. consumers value its product more than the cost of inputs.
    C. consumers value its product more than the labor that produces it.

6. MC: Total revenue is:
    A. opportunity costs minus profits.
    B. price times quantity sold.
    C. accounting profit minus quantity demanded.

7. T/F: If total revenue exceeds total cost, consumers value the product more than the next best use of the inputs.

8. MC: Generally, a business owner's decisions are based on:
    A. certain knowledge.
    B. economists' graphs.
    C. expectations.

9. T/F: Losses discourage the unproductive use of resources.

10. MC: Consumers base their purchasing decisions on:
    A. price and marginal utility.
    B. their knowledge of all the possible alternative uses of resources that went into a product.
    C. the seller's cost of production.

Short Answer

1. How is the cost of inputs determined?
2. How do entrepreneurs' expectations about profits and losses channel resources? What happens when those expectations don't pan out?
3. What does it mean to allocate resources efficiently?

Lecture 10

INCOME AND VALUE

Vocabulary

(Open book: Students should use the glossary at the back of the book, as well as a dictionary, to identify the correct answers. Format: matching)

Value	Not in the form of money
Economic efficiency	Someone who takes risks and brings new products or services to the market
Entrepreneur	A condition in which all actions for which the benefits exceed the cost are taken, and no actions for which the cost exceeds the benefits are taken
Non-monetary	The importance, worth, or usefulness of something

Quiz

(Closed book)

1. MC: People earn income by:
    - A. doing what they love.
    - B. improving other people's lives.
    - C. caring more about others than themselves.

2. MC: According to Pope St. John Paul II, working for income is:
    - A. a way of selflessly caring for others.
    - B. a necessary evil.
    - C. a way of expressing and fulfilling yourself.

3. T/F: Each person has an obligation to earn the highest income possible.

4. MC: How did Mark Zuckerberg get to be so rich?
   A. by taking advantage of other people
   B. by giving many millions of people something that improves their lives
   C. by being very lucky

5. MC: A person's income is a measure of:
   A. how much value the person provides for others.
   B. that person's dignity and worth.
   C. how selfish the person is.

6. According to St. Josemaría Escrivá, "______, for the vast majority of people implies ______ their work."
   A. Sacrifice, sacrificing
   B. Life, living for
   C. Sanctity, sanctifying

7. MC: Higher-paying careers often:
   A. have high opportunity costs.
   B. produce nothing of value.
   C. are more dignified.

8. Information about which careers do most to benefit others is generally provided by:
   A. earning opportunities in different occupations.
   B. career counselors.
   C. common sense.

9. T/F: Pope John Paul II and Adam Smith had very different views about helping yourself by helping others.

10. T/F: People who don't care about improving the world will nevertheless have a strong incentive to develop skills and take actions that are valuable to others.

Short Answer

1. What are some things you should do if your goal is to earn a high income? What are some costs and benefits of pursuing this goal?
2. What are some examples of non-monetary compensation?
3. Why do movie stars earn far more than teachers?

Section 11

Invisible Hand

Vocabulary

(Open book: Students should use the glossary at the back of the book, as well as a dictionary, to identify the correct answers. Format: matching)

Invisible hand	An economic system characterized by collective or governmental ownership and administration of the means of production and distribution of goods
Capitalism	An abstract concept that encompasses the trading arrangements of buyers and sellers that underlie the forces of supply and demand
Socialism	The tendency of market prices to direct individuals pursuing their own self-interest into activities that pro-mote the economic well-being of the society
Market	An economic system characterized by private or corporate ownership of capital goods, by investments that are determined by private decision, and by prices, production, and the distribution of goods that are determined mainly by competition in a free market

Quiz

(Closed book)

1. MC: ______ carries information about consumer preferences, costs, and matters related to timing, location, and circumstance, and registers the choices of millions of consumers, producers, and resource suppliers.
    A. A supercomputer
    B. A technical manual
    C. The price

2. MC: The invisible hand directs self-interest toward:
    A. general prosperity.
    B. empathy.
    C. collective action.

3. T/F: No central authority could possibly get all the information they need to accomplish an efficient allocation of resources.

4. MC: The price system is a feature of:
    A. the free market.
    B. central planning.
    C. socialism.

5. MC: Different economic systems create different:
    A. realities.
    B. demand.
    C. incentives.

6. MC: Incentives in a free market system are created by:
    A. governments.
    B. prices.
    C. rules.

7. MC: A price is a signal wrapped in:
    A. noise.
    B. an enigma.
    C. an incentive.

8. MC: Prices help buyers and sellers adjust to:
    A. economic laws.
    B. changing circumstances.
    C. central authority.

9. T/F: Pope St. John Paul II noted the importance of a system that harnesses individual self-interest to serve the interests of others.

10. In a free market system:
    A. all trades are made where the benefits exceed the costs, and none where costs exceed the benefits.
    B. resources, goods, and services are channeled to the people who value them most.
    C. both A and B.

Short Answer

What information is contained in a price? How and why do people act on this information?

How is it possible to have an orderly economy in which producers' and consumers' activities are coordinated without a central planner? What would happen if we had central planning?

What are some other names for a free-market economic system? What are some kinds of centrally planned economic systems?

Suggested Reading

"I, Pencil" by Leonard Read

Lecture 12

Unintended Consequences

Vocabulary

(Open book: Students should use the glossary at the back of the book, as well as a dictionary, to identify the correct answers. Format: matching)

Great Depression	An official order or command
Secondary effects	A tax on goods imported into a country
Mandate	A course of action undertaken by the government with the aim of achieving a particular goal
Tariffs	The longest and most severe economic downturn in modern history, lasting throughout the 1930s
Import quota	Consequences of a change that are not immediately identifiable but are felt only with the passage of time
Public policy	A specific limit or maximum quantity or value of a good that is permitted to be imported into a country during a given period

Quiz

(Closed book)

1. MC: The belief that destroying goods brings greater wealth is sometimes called the:
   - A. first-order fallacy.
   - B. broken-window fallacy.
   - C. secondary effect.

2. MC: Greater fuel efficiency for cars and light trucks make additional driving:
   - A. safer.
   - B. cheaper.
   - C. faster.

3. MC: Knowing the unintended consequences of fuel efficiency requirements:
    A. tells us that the requirements are bad policy.
    B. tells us the requirements are good policy.
    C. gives us information to weigh costs against benefits.

4. MC: Which of the following would be an unintended consequence of a state increasing its cigarette tax?
    A. state tax revenue increasing
    B. people smoking less
    C. people going to another state to buy cigarettes

5. MC: Sugar quotas:
    A. increase jobs in the US sugar industry.
    B. decrease jobs in the US sugar industry.
    C. have no net effect on employment in the US sugar industry.

6. MC: The effects we are most likely to see and perceive are:
    A. direct effects.
    B. indirect effects.
    C. secondary effects.

7. MC: Destruction from a hurricane:
    A. makes the community worse off, because valuable property was destroyed, and no money was added to the economy.
    B. makes the community better off because it generates construction jobs.
    C. leaves the community neither better nor worse, because everything that was destroyed can be replaced.

8. MC: Thinking like an economist can help you foresee:
    A. all effects of a decision.
    B. certain unintended effects of a decision.
    C. marginal costs of a decision.

9. MC: Often, unintended consequences result from creating bad:
    A. incentives.
    B. demand.
    C. supply.

10. T/F: Trade restrictions reshuffle employment rather than increase it.

Short Answer

1. What does the broken window fallacy ignore?
2. What is the difference between a first- and second-order effect, or a direct and indirect effect?
3. Does the invisible hand involve unseen, unintended consequences? How would you compare the invisible hand to the unintended consequences presented in this chapter?

Lecture 13

Introduction to Living Standards

Vocabulary

(Open book: Students should use the glossary at the back of the book, as well as a dictionary, to identify the correct answers. Format: matching)

Living standard	Defined by the World Bank as living on less than $1.90 per day
Extreme or absolute poverty	Material well-being
Gross domestic product (GDP)	Persistent increases in per capita income and improvements in the standard of living
GDP per capita:	The market value of all goods and services in their final (rather than intermediate) use that are produced within a country during a specific period. It is a measure of both income and output.
Economic prosperity	A country's economic output per person

Quiz

(Closed book)

1. MC: According to Adam Smith, what is the sole end and purpose of production?
   A. job creation
   B. consumption
   C. happiness

2. T/F: Living standards includes consumption goods but excludes services such as education and medical care.

3. MC: Living standards increase when a society:
   A. increases production of things people value.
   B. destroys products that people value.
   C. creates more jobs.

4. MC: Populations are rising primarily in:
   A. countries with higher GDP per capita.
   B. less developed countries.
   C. the most developed countries.

5. MC: In recent decades, extreme poverty worldwide has:
   A. increased.
   B. decreased.
   C. stayed flat.

6. MC: The 1933 Agricultural Adjustment Act:
   A. paid farmers to destroy food.
   B. has led to a decline in extreme poverty.
   C. raised the living standards of most Americans.

7. MC: Higher GDP per capita is correlated with:
   A. happiness.
   B. spiritual well-being.
   C. satisfaction with living standards.

8. T/F: Worldwide, child mortality has increased in recent decades.

9. MC: The Cash for Clunkers program:
   A. caused a long-term increase in new car sales by offering subsidies.
   B. caused the prices of used cars to increase by decreasing the supply.
   C. caused general prosperity to increase by destroying marketable goods.

10. MC: Government policies that block opportunities to work or enter certain industries:
   A. increase living standards.
   B. increase wealth.
   C. fail to increase living standards.

Short Answer

1. What are some ways in which your life is better off than it would be if you lived in a much less productive economy?
2. Why doesn't it make sense to use hand tools to build a dam instead of using modern machinery if using hand tools would create more jobs?
3. Who is helped by government policies that reduce production of particular goods or services? Why can't such a policy raise general living standards?
4. What did Pope John Paul II mean by "idolatry of the market"?

Suggested Enrichment Activities

1. Watch "Hans Rosling's 200 Countries, 200 Years, 4 Minutes – The Joy of Stats – BBC Four," https://www.youtube.com/watch?v=jbkSRLYSojo.
2. Explore Animated Data with Gapminder: https://www.gapminder.org/tools.

Lecture 14

Sources of Economic Progress

Vocabulary

(Open book: Students should use the glossary at the back of the book, as well as a dictionary, to identify the correct answers. Format: matching)

Physical capital	An increase in the production of goods and services in an economy
Human capital	The public policies that govern the economy
Economic rules (economic organization)	Human-made resources such as tools, equipment, and structures
Economic growth (economic progress)	The purchase, construction, or development of capital resources, including both nonhuman and human capital
Investment	The abilities, skills, and health of human beings that contribute to the production of both current and future output

Quiz

(Closed book)

1. MC: The question of what causes _________ was the topic of the book that launched economics as its own field.
   - A. trade
   - B. economic growth
   - C. marginal utility

2. MC: Mass production allows economies of:
   - A. supply and demand.
   - B. markets.
   - C. scale.

3. T/F: Economic rules influence the other causes of economic growth.

4. MC: Adding more machines usually requires the ability to:
   A. borrow money.
   B. manage expectations.
   C. consider unintended consequences.

5. MC: An example of an economic rule, as the phrase is used in this lesson, is:
   A. a stable currency.
   B. the law of demand.
   C. transportation and communication technology.

6. MC: Entrepreneurs take ______ in the hope of profit.
   A. security
   B. risks
   C. heed

7. T/F: Investments in capital lead to increased worker productivity.

8. MC: One of the first inventions that reduced our reliance on human and animal energy was:
   A. the steam engine.
   B. nuclear power.
   C. the rule of law.

9. MC: Education is a way to create:
   A. physical capital.
   B. human capital.
   C. capitalism.

10. MC: Electricity, the internet, and 5G are examples of:
    A. investments in human capital.
    B. improved economic organization.
    C. improved technology.

Short Answer

1. What are three ways technology brings about economic growth?
2. What is an entrepreneur's role in boosting economic growth?
3. In previous lessons we learned about the gains from trade and the importance of reducing transaction costs. What are the additional sources of economic progress covered in this lesson?

Lecture 15

LEGAL SYSTEM

Vocabulary

(Open book: Students should use the glossary at the back of the book, as well as a dictionary, to identify the correct answers. Format: matching)

Private property rights	The rights to exclusive use, legal protection against invaders, and the right to transfer to others
Productivity	The average output produced per worker during a specific time period, usually measured as output per hour worked
Rule of law	The authority and influence of law in society; the principle whereby all members of a society (including those in government) are considered equally subject to publicly disclosed legal codes and processes.
Public policy	A course of action undertaken by the government with the aim of achieving a particular goal

Quiz
(Closed book)

1. MC: Private ownership of property involves the right to _______ use, legal protection against invaders, and the right to transfer the property to others.
   - A. fair
   - B. exclusive
   - C. efficient

2. MC: If people fail to care for their private property, they bear the consequence in the form of:
   - A. government crackdown.
   - B. declining property value.
   - C. declining incomes.

3. MC: Property rights allow people to keep:
    A. the fruits of their labor.
    B. their jobs.
    C. common ownership of housing.

4. MC: In the USSR, private plots produced a fourth of all agricultural output and consisted of:
    A. 2 percent of the land under cultivation.
    B. a fourth of all land under cultivation.
    C. half of all land under cultivation.

5. MC: Agricultural productivity in China increased when the government began allowing farmers to keep all that they produced beyond:
    A. the amount grown on private plots.
    B. a quota given to the state.
    C. their subsistence needs.

6. MC: Private property owners have incentive to conserve whenever the future expected value of a resource exceeds:
    A. zero.
    B. accounting profit.
    C. current consumption value.

7. MC: As whale oil prices rose:
    A. people curtailed hunting to conserve the resource.
    B. people curtailed hunting because of government regulation.
    C. entrepreneurs developed substitute oil sources.

8. MC: With contract enforcement under the rule of law, people know that:
    A. government is watching them closely.
    B. others will likely keep their agreements.
    C. courts will favor big business.

9. MC: When increasing scarcity causes the price of a privately-owned resource to rise:
    A. people will have the incentive to conserve on the use of the resource, find substitutes, and find new ways to extract more of the resource.
    B. people will have the incentive to use as much of the resource as they can before it runs out.
    C. people will recognize the benefits of communal ownership.

10. T/F: Doomsday forecasts are often wrong because they fail to consider the incentives that flow from private ownership.

Short Answer

1. In what three ways does a good legal system support economic progress?
2. What are the four kinds of incentives owners have in a system of private property rights that lead to economic growth?
3. Give an example not used in the book or lecture of each of the four types of incentives from question 2.
4. How can ownership of property provide an incentive for an owner to conserve even beyond his or her expected lifespan?

Lecture 16

Competitive Markets

Vocabulary

(Open book: Students should use the glossary at the back of the book, as well as a dictionary, to identify the correct answers. Format: matching)

Innovation	An economic system characterized by private or corporate ownership of capital goods, by investments that are determined by private decision, and by prices, production, and the distribution of goods that are de-termined mainly by competition in a free market
Investor	Someone who takes risks and brings new products or services to the market
Entrepreneur	Someone who provides a business with capital, with the expectation of a future financial gain
Capitalism	A new method, product, or idea

Quiz

(Closed book)

1. MC: At the most basic level, what creates competition is:
   A. a market economy.
   B. entrepreneurs.
   C. scarcity.

2. MC: Competition is present only when:
   A. there are multiple companies in a market.
   B. different companies charge different prices.
   C. alternative sellers are free to enter a market.

3. T/F: In a free market, buyers compete with sellers.

4. MC: Which techniques will work best is something:
    A. well-known by any business owner who has studied economics.
    B. competition allows us to discover.
    C. we can calculate using equations.

5. MC: Entrepreneurs need only the support of ________ to try their ideas
    A. investors
    B. accountants
    C. economists

6. MC: In a free market, competition motivates businesses to:
    A. cut corners on quality.
    B. produce inefficiently.
    C. develop new products.

7. MC: Initial purchasers:
    A. get the best price/quality deal.
    B. pay dearly for early availability.
    C. are mostly low-income.

8. MC: Creative destruction refers to:
    A. an innovation that makes something obsolete.
    B. self-interest harnessed to improve society.
    C. businesses using their size to block competitors.

9. MC: What prevents a business from charging high prices, selling shoddy products, and providing bad service?
    A. government regulations
    B. their employees
    C. competition

10. T/F: Businesses do not like to face competition, and they commonly lobby for policies to protect themselves from it.

Short Answer

1. How do initial purchasers of innovative technology help later purchasers?
2. Why do large companies thrive in some sectors and much smaller ones in others?
3. How does competition in a free market system channel goods and resources to those who value them most?
4. Besides low prices, what are some other ways businesses offer value to consumers?

Lecture 17

Limits on Regulation

Vocabulary

(Open book: Students should use the glossary at the back of the book, as well as a dictionary, to identify the correct answers. Format: matching)

Monopoly	Highly profitable
Oligopoly	Confirms the education, training, and other qualifications of an individual, but does not prohibit noncerti-fied individuals from competing in the market
Discretion	A market characterized by a single seller of a well-defined product for which there are no good substitutes; and high barriers to the entry of any other firms into the market for that product
Lucrative	The power or right to decide or act according to one's own judgment
Proponent	A state of limited competition, in which a market is shared by a small number of producers or sellers
Certification	A requirement that a person obtain permission from the government in order to perform certain business activities or work in certain occupations
Occupational licensing	Advocate, supporter

Quiz

(Closed book)

1. MC: Government restrictions on entry into a market can lead to:
    - A. monarchy or oligarchy.
    - B. monopoly or oligopoly.
    - C. more competitive markets.
2. MC: Some regulations weaken the rule of law by giving ________ to government authorities.
    - A. raises
    - B. monopoly
    - C. discretion
3. MC: Price floors create excess:
    - A. supply.
    - B. demand.
    - C. money.
4. MC: Regulations creating a long process for legally opening a business are an example of:
    - A. barriers to entry.
    - B. the rule of law.
    - C. price controls.
5. MC: The minimum wage is an example of:
    - A. occupational licensing.
    - B. a price control.
    - C. crony capitalism.
6. MC: Price controls keeping the market price from adjusting to the efficient equilibrium is:
    - A. a deliberate goal of the policy.
    - B. a secondary effect of the policy.
    - C. a means for increasing exchange.
7. MC: Rent control is an example of a:
    - A. price floor.
    - B. barrier to entry.
    - C. price ceiling.
8. T/F: Crony capitalism is the same thing as capitalism.
9. T/F: Economic thinking can help identify ways to pursue the goal of a living wage that are less disruptive to economic progress than minimum wage laws.

10. MC: Interior decorator licensing requirements are an example of government regulations that:
    A. undermine the rule of law.
    B. prevent prices from adjusting freely.
    C. restrict sellers from entering a market.

Short Answer

1. What are three ways government regulations reduce the gains from trade and competition?
2. Why do existing sellers often support government restrictions on entry into a market?
3. How do price controls prevent the market from adjusting to the equilibrium price?
4. Why do regulations that let government make decisions on a case-by-case basis weaken the rule of law?
5. What can economics allow us to predict about the effects of the minimum wage? What are its positive effects? What are its negative effects?
6. What are some reasons a minimum wage is not effective at reducing poverty?

Lecture 18

Efficient Capital Market

Vocabulary

(Open book: Students should use the glossary at the back of the book, as well as a dictionary, to identify the correct answers. Format: matching)

Capital investment	A situation in which the allocation of resources and capital is substantially influenced by political decision-making rather than by market forces
Investment goods or capital goods	The markets for stocks, bonds, and real estate
Consumer goods	A reduction in current consumption in order to make the funds available for other uses
Saving	Goods produced for present use
Capital market	Goods or facilities bought or constructed for the purpose of producing future economic benefits
Crony capitalism	Expenditure on buildings, machinery, tools, and other equipment that will enhance future productivity

Quiz

(Closed book)

1. MC: Investment increases ________ consumption but requires forgoing _______ consumption.
   - A. efficient, wasteful
   - B. future, present
   - C. marginal, conspicuous

2. MC: The interest rate rewards:
    A. delayed gratification.
    B. homebuyers.
    C. hard work.

3. MC: The interest rate is the _______ of loanable funds.
    A. quantity demanded
    B. investment
    C. price

4. MC: Who are the suppliers in the capital market?
    A. savers, mostly households
    B. businesses seeking to construct capital projects
    C. payday lenders

5. MC: Thomas Edison was able to produce his inventions because:
    A. he inherited a fortune from his grandfather.
    B. he had access to a competitive banking system.
    C. he had political connections.

6. T/F: Investment rates in the Soviet Union were among the lowest in the world.

7. MC: _______ ensure that the flow of capital to counterproductive projects is eventually cut off.
    A. Profits
    B. Losses
    C. Interest rates

8. T/F: Interest rates for a project vary based on the supply and demand in the loanable funds market as well as factors specific to that particular investment.

9. MC: ______________________ will channel resources away from unsuccessful projects and toward more successful ones.
    A. Government planners
    B. Competitive capital markets
    C. Crony capitalism

10. MC: Through Fannie Mae and Freddie Mac, government policy on housing lending:
    A. helped generate an increase in home ownership and an increase in home prices.
    B. eventually led to a steep increase in mortgage defaults and foreclosures.
    C. both A and B.

Short Answer

1. Why is the accumulation of capital important for economic growth?
2. How did Fannie Mae and Freddie Mac intentionally allocate capital differently from how a private capital market would have done so?

Lecture 19

Monetary Stability

Vocabulary

(Open book: Students should use the glossary at the back of the book, as well as a dictionary, to identify the correct answers. Format: matching)

Money	The supply of currency and checking account funds in a country
Money supply	A general increase in the price level
Medium of exchange	Anything that is generally accepted as final payment for goods and services by buyers and sellers
Monetary policy	A measure of value in terms of which accounts are kept and values stated
Inflation	A form of money issued by a government and declared to be legal tender. This type of currency is not linked to any asset of value and can be printed at will by central governments.
Unit of account	Any item that is widely acceptable in exchange for goods and services
Fiat currency	The deliberate control of the national money supply and, in some cases, credit conditions, by the government

Quiz

(Closed book)

1. MC: Money ________ value.
    A. lacks
    B. stores
    C. destroys

2. T/F: Money is a common unit of value that the value of all goods and services can be converted into.

3. MC: Money reduces:
   A. interest rates.
   B. marginal utility.
   C. transaction costs.

4. MC: High inflation discourages:
   A. saving and investment.
   B. consumption.
   C. bartering.

5. T/F: Increasing the money supply increases prices.

6. MC: Monetary policy seeks to:
   A. keep the supply of gold stable.
   B. counteract booms and busts.
   C. keep interest rates consistently low.

7. MC: Which of the following are *not* features of a good currency?
   A. portability and durability
   B. uniformity and acceptability
   C. indivisibility and variability

8. MC: The value of money is determined by:
   A. supply and demand.
   B. fiat.
   C. the Dow Jones Industrial Average.

9. When the supply of money expands rapidly compared to _______, the value of money declines.
   A. the supply of goods and services
   B. interest rates
   C. the supply of gold

10. When the value of money declines, prices:
   A. fall.
   B. rise.
   C. stay the same.

Short Answer

1. What are three purposes of money?
2. List the features of a good currency. Which would make a better currency: books or strings of shells? Explain why.
3. What happens when there is more money in circulation but the same amount of goods and services as before?
4. Why do high and variable rates of inflation undermine prosperity?

Optional

Reading/listening: "Functions of Money," Federal Reserve Bank of St. Louis, https://www.stlouisfed.org/education/economic-lowdown-podcast-series/episode-9-functions-of-money.

Watching: "Zimbabwe and Hyperinflation: Who Wants to Be a Trillionaire?" Marginal Revolution University, https://www.youtube.com/watch?v=78-BlZXm7wA.

Lecture 20

Low Tax Rates

Vocabulary

(Open book: Students should use the glossary at the back of the book, as well as a dictionary, to identify the correct answers. Format: matching)

Progressive income taxes	The tax rate incurred on each additional dollar of income
Marginal tax rate	A factor that discourages people from doing something
Disincentive	A situation in which someone benefits without having to make a fair contribution
Perverse incentive	A tax in which the tax rate increases as the taxable amount increases
Free ride	An incentive that has an unintended and undesirable result that is contrary to the intentions of its designers. A type of negative unintended consequence.

Quiz

(Closed book)

1. MC: In the US, our income tax system is:
   A. progressive.
   B. flat rate.
   C. regressive.

2. MC: It is the ________________ tax rate that matters when people are deciding how much to work.
   A. average
   B. total
   C. marginal

3. T/F: High marginal tax rates artificially increase the cost, to the consumer, of tax-deductible items.

4. T/F: The disincentive effects of high marginal tax rates are only a major issue for those with high earnings.

5. MC: For some ________ transactions, taxes will turn them from net beneficial to net costly.
   A. marginal
   B. wasteful
   C. complicated

6. In 2020, the top marginal federal income tax rate was:
   A. 17 percent.
   B. 37 percent.
   C. 57 percent.

7. MC: Tax shelters:
   A. avoid the costs that taxes impose on society.
   B. lead people to waste scarce capital.
   C. are widely used when marginal tax rates are low

Use the table below of 2020 US income tax rates to answer questions 8-10 about someone earning $90,000 per year.

Rate	For Single Individuals
10%	Up to $9,875
12%	$9,876 to $40,125
22%	$40,126 to $85,525
24%	$85,526 to $163,300
32%	$163,301 to $207,350
35%	$207,351 to $518,400
37%	$518,401 or more

8. Calculate how much tax the individual will pay on the on the portion of their income that falls into each of the first three tax brackets. (Round to the nearest dollar.)

9. How much tax will this person pay on the last $4,475 in income?

10. Calculate this person's total tax. What is their average tax rate? What is their marginal tax rate?

Short Answer

1. How can a higher marginal income tax rate affect people's willingness provide more value to others?
2. In what four ways do higher income tax rates harm the economy?
3. For what reasons can some of the government spending paid for by taxes be beneficial?

Lecture 21

Free Trade

Vocabulary

(Open book: Students should use the glossary at the back of the book, as well as a dictionary, to identify the correct answers. Format: matching)

Exchange rate	Individuals, firms, regions, or nations can produce a larger output and achieve mutual gains from trade by specializing in the production of goods they can produce at low opportunity cost
Subsidiarity	Reductions in the firm's per-unit costs that occur when large factories are used to produce large volumes of output
Solidarity	The process of concentrating on and becoming expert in a particular subject or skill
Specialization	Mutual support and care among people; a commitment to the common good
Economies of scale	A principle of social organization that holds that social and political issues should be dealt with at the most immediate (or local) level that is consistent with their resolution
Law of comparative advantage	The rate at which one currency will be exchanged for another; also, the value of one country's currency in relation to another currency

Quiz

(Closed book)

1. MC: Countries with abundant land and sparse populations tend to specialize in:
   - A. beef and wheat.
   - B. cameras and computers.
   - C. services.

2. T/F: Trade restrictions neither create nor destroy jobs; they reshuffle them.

3. MC: International trade allows us to take fuller advantage of:
   A. gross domestic product.
   B. tax shelters.
   C. economies of scale.

4. MC: Holding down the value of domestic currency in exchange with foreigners:
   A. encourages imports and discourages exports.
   B. encourages exports and discourages imports.
   C. discourages both imports and exports.

5. T/F: The US has a policy of complete free trade.

6. MC: Our living standards are determined by:
   A. the availability of goods and services.
   B. the number of jobs in the economy.
   C. the level of exports relative to imports.

7. MC: Pope John Paul II noted the importance of the global economy:
   A. maximizing consumption.
   B. promoting economies of scale.
   C. being open to people in developing nations.

8. MC: Free trade policies in developed countries often increase demand for:
   A. high-skilled labor relative to low-skilled.
   B. money relative to goods and services.
   C. investment relative to consumption.

9. MC: Policy makers must weigh the benefits of international trade to domestic consumers against:
   A. the benefits to people in foreign countries.
   B. job losses in some high-cost domestic industries.
   C. the size of the trade deficit.

10. T/F: International trade is more beneficial to people in high-wage countries than in low-wage countries.

Short Answer

1. What are three reasons countries can benefit from international trade?
2. Why can free trade increase income inequality within a high-income country? Why does it decrease worldwide income inequality?
3. How does international trade allow us to benefit from different countries' different resource endowments?
4. What are three key principles of the Catholic perspective on trade?

Lecture 22

Introduction to Public Choice

Vocabulary

(Open book: Students should use the glossary at the back of the book, as well as a dictionary, to identify the correct answers. Format: matching)

Economic efficiency	A system whereby the government undertakes to protect the health and well-being of its citizens, especial-ly those in financial or social need, by means of grants, pensions, and other benefits
Authoritarian regime	The public policies that govern the economy
Autonomy	The study of decision-making as it affects the formation and operation of collective organizations such as governments. In general the principles and methodology of economies are applied to political science top-ics.
Welfare state	A situation in which all activities generating more benefit than cost are undertaken and no activities are undertaken for which the cost exceeds the benefit
Economic rules (economic organization)	Any political system that concentrates power in the hands of a leader or a small elite that is not constitu-tionally responsible to the body of the people
Public choice analysis	Independence or freedom; the right of self-government

Quiz

(Closed book)

1. MC: In the US, government expenditures now constitute __________ of national income.
    - A. 25 percent
    - B. 40 percent
    - C. 70 percent

2. T/F: Economic thinking applies only to economic decisions.

3. MC: Catholic social teaching:
    - A. identifies ideals and principles.
    - B. advocates specific government policies.
    - C. helps us understand the incentives of politicians and interest groups.

4. MC: The Catholic Church has historically advocated:
    - A. socialism.
    - B. free markets.
    - C. a middle way between socialism and free markets.

5. MC: Popes have held that the state has the duty of:
    - A. watching over the common good.
    - B. solving every social problem.
    - C. interceding between the individual and family.

6. T/F: There is no "middle way" between free markets and socialism.

7. MC: According to John Paul II, the welfare state could be good because it:
    - A. eliminates the role of self-interest.
    - B. remedies poverty.
    - C. increases state power.

8. MC: According to John Paul II, the welfare state can do harm by:
    - A. departing from a pure free market.
    - B. violating subsidiarity.
    - C. limiting the autonomy of businesspeople.

9. MC: Public choice economics:
    - A. applies economic thinking to the political realm.
    - B. applies political thinking to the economic realm.
    - C. both A and B.

10. T/F: Understanding the role of incentives in politics can help explain political outcomes.

Short Answer

1. How do political systems affect economic systems?
2. According to John Paul II, what does the principle of solidarity require of governments?

Optional Reading

Centesimus Annus http://www.vatican.va/content/john-paul-ii/en/encyclicals/documents/hf_jp-ii_enc_01051991_centesimus-annus.html.

Lecture 23

MARKET INEFFICIENCIES

Vocabulary

(Open book: Students should use the glossary at the back of the book, as well as a dictionary, to identify the correct answers. Format: matching)

Barriers to entry	Goods that are a) jointly consumed and b) nonexcludable
Merger	A company's ability to manipulate the price of an item in the marketplace by manipulating the level of sup-ply
Collusion	Spillover effects that impose a cost or benefit on those who are not involved in the transaction
Market power	A combination of two or more companies into one larger company
Public goods	An agreement between firms that usually compete against each other to set the prices for their goods in order to gain an advantage
Externalities	Obstacles that make it difficult for new companies to enter a given market (e.g., high fixed costs, government regulations, or patents)

Quiz

(Closed book)

1. MC: Which of the following market conditions encourages innovation and promotes efficiency?
   - A. monopoly
   - B. competition
   - C. collusion

2. MC: A monopoly can arise if there are:
   - A. high transaction costs.
   - B. diminishing marginal utilities.
   - C. strong economies of scale.

3. T/F: For public goods, one person's consumption doesn't leave less for someone else.

4. MC: The protective function:
   A. is provided by the free market in non-communist countries.
   B. fails to enhance the welfare of the citizenry.
   C. includes rules against theft and fraud.

5. T/F: With public goods, price signals tell government when the benefits of additional production exceed the costs.

6. MC: Public goods are:
   A. jointly consumed and non-excludable.
   B. individually consumed and excludable.
   C. non-excludable and profitable.

7. MC: A monopoly may profit by:
   A. restricting output.
   B. providing public goods.
   C. undercutting the competition.

8. MC: Spillover effects of an individual's actions are called:
   A. public goods.
   B. externalities.
   C. protection function.

9. MC: A free market will:
   A. overproduce goods that have negative externalities.
   B. overproduce goods that have positive externalities.
   C. underproduce goods that have negative externalities.

10. MC: My neighbor removing trees that were blocking my view of the ocean is an example of:
    A. a public good.
    B. a negative externality.
    C. a positive externality.

Short Answer

1. What are three ways government can help the economy?
2. What are the two major categories of market inefficiency?
3. What are the two sources of monopoly power?
4. What can government do about positive and negative externalities? Why is the existence of positive externalities a "problem" that needs solving?

Lecture 24

Political Decision-Making

Vocabulary

(Open book: Students should use the glossary at the back of the book, as well as a dictionary, to identify the correct answers. Format: matching)

Dispersed	Trying to increase one's share of existing wealth without creating new wealth; attempts by individuals or groups to influence public policy to redistribute more income to themselves
Special interest group	Choosing to be uninformed about an issue because the cost of becoming informed is greater than the po-tential benefit
Lobbying	The exchange between politicians of political support on one issue for political support on another
Logrolling	Lawfully seeking to influence the actions, policies, or decisions of government officials
Rational ignorance	An organization of people united by a common interest
Rent seeking	Spread out or distributed broadly

Quiz

(Closed book)

1. MC: The allocation of resources through the democratic process:
   A. makes it possible for the majority to coerce the minority.
   B. prevents some from benefiting at the expense of others.
   C. is the ideal form of economic organization.

2. MC: Government failure occurs when the __________ of political participants encourage(s) counterproductive use of resources.
   A. morality
   B. incentives
   C. knowledge

3. MC: The framers of the Constitution called special-interest groups:
    - A. crony capitalists.
    - B. federalists.
    - C. factions.

4. MC: Concentrated benefits and dispersed costs means _________________ have stronger incentives to be informed about policy than the average voter does.
    - A. politicians
    - B. special interest groups
    - C. rational voters

5. MC: Taking the time to research sugar subsidies in hopes of informing a voting decision to benefit themselves would, for most voters, be:
    - A. beyond their mental capacity.
    - B. too selfish.
    - C. irrational.

6. T/F: Public choice economics predicts that politicians will prefer deficit financing over raising taxes.

7. The way for an interest group to obtain government funds is usually to:
    - A. openly advocate plundering others.
    - B. tie its interest to popular objectives.
    - C. overcome the rational ignorance of the electorate.

8. Wealth transfers lead people to costly actions to:
    - A. qualify for the transfer.
    - B. sacrifice for the greater good.
    - C. pay their debts.

9. T/F: When the benefits are concentrated on a small group and the costs dispersed across a large number of people, policies can be adopted that are a net loss.

10. MC: The actual behavior of our elected representatives is generally:
    - A. to adopt rational ignorance.
    - B. to adopt broadly beneficial policies in the interests of their constituents.
    - C. to adopt policies that benefit special interests.

Short Answer

1. What three questions should we ask when using economic thinking to identify incentives in politics?
2. How are the answers to the above questions different when we're identifying incentives in the free market versus in politics?
3. How can it be rational for voters to remain ignorant?
4. Why can a democracy encourage politicians to support the interests of a small special-interest group instead of a majority?
5. What problems can a high debt-to-GDP ratio create for a country?

Optional Reading

"Lobbying Data Summary," Center for Responsive Politics, https://www.opensecrets.org/federal-lobbying.

Lecture 25

Economic Systems

Vocabulary

(Open book: Students should use the glossary at the back of the book, as well as a dictionary, to identify the correct answers. Format: matching)

Command and control	A resource that benefits a group of people, but which provides diminished benefits to everyone if each in-dividual pursues his or her own self-interest
Common pool resource	Controlled by state and local authorities rather than by the federal government
Industrial policy	An economic system in which government central planners control the means of production and determine the distribution of output
Decentralized	Organized government involvement in guiding the economy by encouraging investment in targeted industries

Quiz

(Closed book)

1. MC: Politicians and central planners make decisions based on:
   - A. their own preferences.
   - B. pursuit of power.
   - C. both A and B.

2. MC: Individuals in the market make decisions based on:
   - A. their own utility.
   - B. zero-sum transactions.
   - C. both A and B.

3. MC: Catholic Social Teaching leaves it to decision-makers' judgment:
   A. what goals to pursue.
   B. how best to pursue Catholic ideals.
   C. how to convert people to Catholicism.

4. MC: Government agencies pursue:
   A. higher budgets from legislatures.
   B. sales to customers.
   C. profits for investors.

5. MC: What prevents private companies, but not usually government programs, from continuously wasting money?
   A. bankruptcy
   B. social conscience
   C. central planning

6. T/F: In a free market, individual decision-makers have the incentive to only do things whose benefits exceed the costs.

7. MC: A government's budget is similar to a ________ resource.
   A. commonly-owned
   B. natural
   C. renewable

8. MC: Competition among governments works best when there is:
   A. democracy.
   B. decentralization.
   C. a principle of motion.

9. T/F: Politicians and central planners have the incentive to support successful projects that will increase wealth for society.

10. MC: It is the information conveyed through ________________ that informs investors, firms, and workers where their dollars and efforts create the most value for others.
   A. prices
   B. government agencies
   C. the third way

Short Answer

1. What makes the economy too complex to be centrally planned?
2. What did the man of system fail to understand about people, according to Adam Smith?
3. How might public choice analysis show the difficulty of ensuring fairness even with a "middle way" of economic rules?

Lecture 26

Introduction to Personal Finance

Vocabulary

(Open book: Students should use the glossary at the back of the book, as well as a dictionary, to identify the correct answers. Format: matching)

Risk	A legal agreement by which a creditor lends money at interest in exchange for taking title of the debtor's property until the debt is repaid
Return	The interest rate adjusted for inflation; it indicates the real cost to the borrower (and yield to the lender) in terms of goods and services
Mortgage	The odds of losing money on an investment
Real interest rate	A measure of the profit or loss of an investment over time as a percentage of the original investment

Quiz

(Closed book)

1. MC: The principle of ________________ explains why you can benefit from specialization in things you do best.
    - A. marginal utility
    - B. comparative advantage
    - C. the invisible hand
2. MC: Life is about:
    - A. choices.
    - B. making money.
    - C. supply and demand.

3. MC: To achieve high income, pursue:
   A. your comparative advantage.
   B. your dreams.
   C. your opportunity cost.

4. MC: In evaluating costs and benefits, ______________ is a complicated consideration.
   A. the price tag
   B. the economic system
   C. time

5. MC: In evaluating financial choices, you face:
   A. temptation.
   B. uncertainty.
   C. supply and demand.

6. MC: If you come to regret a financial decision:
   A. do the opposite next time.
   B. avoid making plans for the future.
   C. consider whether it was bad luck or bad judgment.

7. MC: Borrowing enables __________ for individuals and businesses.
   A. financial growth
   B. unlimited spending
   C. special interests

8. T/F: You should always pay off debt before investing.

9. T/F: In general, the higher the risk, the lower the return.

10. T/F: No matter what our objectives in life, they are easier to achieve if we have more wealth.

Short Answer

1. What is the purpose of taking on debt?
2. What is your opportunity cost for paying down a mortgage early?
3. Why is it important for everyone to have a financial plan?

Lecture 27

EARNINGS

Vocabulary

(Open book: Students should use the glossary at the back of the book, as well as a dictionary, to identify the correct answers. Format: matching)

Value	Not in the form of money
Economic efficiency	The importance, worth, or usefulness of something
Entrepreneur	A condition in which all actions for which the benefits exceed the cost are taken, and no actions for which the cost exceeds the benefits are taken
Non-monetary	Someone who takes risks and brings new products or services to the market

Quiz

(Closed book)

1. MC: _______ career paths are uncommon.
   A. Straight
   B. Rational
   C. Successful

2. MC: You create a track record:
   A. until you've arrived.
   B. that narrows your path.
   C. throughout your career.

3. MC: Having high opportunity costs of taking a job indicates you have:
   A. bad work habits.
   B. good career options.
   C. a victim mentality.

4. MC: According to researcher Arthur Brooks, ___________ is the central element of happiness
    A. money
    B. earned success
    C. entrepreneurship

5. MC: The self-employed account for one-sixth of the labor force but _____________ of America's millionaires.
    A. 1 percent
    B. one-fifth
    C. two-thirds

6. MC: In a cover letter and interview, you should:
    A. tailor your statements to the job.
    B. say the same thing regardless of the job.
    C. say whatever comes to mind.

7. T/F: Entrepreneurial thinking is for business owners, not employees.

8. T/F: Your comparative advantage is determined by your absolute abilities, not your relative abilities.

9. MC: When you are applying for a job, remember that:
    A. you are asking the prospective employer to do you a favor.
    B. you need to show the prospective employer how hiring you would benefit them.
    C. you should keep your answers brief and spend most of the time listening.

10. MC: Develop and document your ability to add value through:
    A. education, training, and experience.
    B. work ethic and entrepreneurial thinking.
    C. both A and B.

Short Answer

1. What are some ways you can enhance future earnings through your performance in your current job?
2. Why is it that, even if you think you're bad at everything or good at everything, you still have a comparative advantage in some specialty?

Optional Watching

"The Surprising Truth About What Motivates Us | Dan Pink," TheNuvoEntrepreneur, YouTube video, https://www.youtube.com/watch?v=KgGhSOAtAyQ.

Section 28

Budgeting

Vocabulary

(Open book: Students should use the glossary at the back of the book, as well as a dictionary, to identify the correct answers. Format: matching)

Budget	The ability of a customer to obtain goods or services before payment, based on the trust that payment will be made in the future
Finance	An asset that can be easily and quickly converted to purchasing power without loss of value
Liquid asset	To obtain money for, often through borrowing
Credit	Estimated income and itemized planned expenditures for a time period

Quiz

(Closed book)

1. MC: You should create a budget and ________ your spending.
   A. cut
   B. minimize
   C. track

2. MC: If you spend more than your budget for a category, you will have to:
   A. cut back on spending.
   B. increase your budget.
   C. A or B.
   D. both A and B.

3. MC: Saving and investing should be:
   A. zero in an economically efficient budget.
   B. a budget category.
   C. whatever is left over from your budget.

4. MC: Credit cards should be:
   A. avoided by almost everyone.
   B. used to build credit and provide liquidity.
   C. used to fund long-term debt.

5. MC: Avoid borrowing to buy something if:
   A. the debt will outlast the product.
   B. you don't absolutely need it.
   C. you are maxed out on your credit card.

6. MC: An unused balance on your credit card:
   A. is extra wealth.
   B. provides additional borrowing power.
   C. is inefficient.

7. MC: Paying down your credit card debt:
   A. is a high-interest investment.
   B. is a huge waste of money.
   C. is futile.

8. T/F: You should always pay down debt before saving and investing.

9. T/F: You can make a budget even if you don't have a steady income.

10. T/F: The goal of budgeting is to help you achieve your financial goals.

Short Answer

1. How does a budget channel your resources?
2. Should exceeding spending in a budget category make you feel bad about yourself? Why or why not?

Lecture 29

Compounding Growth

Vocabulary

(Open book: Students should use the glossary at the back of the book, as well as a dictionary, to identify the correct answers. Format: matching)

Interest	The profit from an investment, as a percentage of the original amount invested
Compound interest	An asset that can be easily and quickly converted to purchasing power without loss of value
Principal	A product offered by banks and credit unions that provides an interest rate premium in exchange for the customer agreeing to leave a lump-sum deposit untouched for a predetermined period of time.
Rate of return	The original amount invested or lent
Liquid asset	A basket of five hundred stocks that are selected because they are thought to be collectively representa-tive of the stock market as a whole
Certificate of Deposit (CD)	Money paid at a particular rate for the use of money lent
Standard and Poor's (S&P) 500 index	Interest that is earned not only on the principal but also on the interest previously earned

Quiz

(Closed book)

1. MC: The alternative to maintaining a rainy-day fund is:
    - A. being unable to meet emergency spending needs.
    - B. borrowing at high interest.
    - C. being careful to avoid emergencies.

2. MC: You should save money because:
   A. you enjoy buying things more when you are old.
   B. you can increase your total consumption that way.
   C. you can live more modestly that way.

3. MC: Compound interest is:
   A. interest on interest.
   B. accounting profit.
   C. for emergencies only.

4. MC: Keeping money in a checking or savings account provides:
   A. liquidity.
   B. high risk.
   C. high return.

5. MC: A retirement fund is for:
   A. liquidity.
   B. consumption.
   C. long-term investment.

6. T/F: You should always avoid high-risk investments.

7. MC: When should you definitely start saving for retirement?
   A. When the expected return makes it worth reducing current spending.
   B. Now
   C. When you have an employer who matches your retirement fund contributions.

8. T/F: Certificates of Deposits (CDs) are more liquid than stocks

9. T/F: You should always pay off all debt before saving and investing.

10. MC: Which debts should you pay off first?
   A. the smallest ones
   B. the ones you owe to friends and family
   C. the highest-interest ones

Short Answer

1. Under what circumstances should you pay off a loan early, and why?
2. What is the reason for starting your saving and investing early? What would be a reason to put off saving and investing until later?

Lecture 30

INVESTING

Vocabulary

(Open book: Students should use the glossary at the back of the book, as well as a dictionary, to identify the correct answers. (Format: matching)

Stock	The holdings of savings, investments, and real assets such as real estate owned by an individual or financial institution
Bond	An entity that pools the funds of investors and channels them into various categories of investments
Principal	The theory that current stock prices already reflect all known information about the future.
Equities	An equity mutual fund that holds a portfolio of stocks that matches their share (or weight) in a broad stock market index such as the S&P 500
Diversification	An equity mutual fund that has a portfolio manager who decides what stocks will be held in the fund and when they will be bought or sold
Portfolio	Ownership shares of a corporation
Mutual fund	The amount of funds borrowed
Managed equity mutual fund	The strategy of investing in a number of diverse firms, industries, and instruments such as stocks, bonds, and real estate in order to minimize the risk accompanying investments
Indexed equity mutual fund	A promise to repay the principal (amount borrowed) plus interest at a specified time in the future
Random walk theory	Shares of stock in a company

Quiz

(Closed book)

1. MC: Stocks entitle you to:
   A. a guaranteed rate of return.
   B. fraction of future revenues.
   C. liability for the company's debts.

2. MC: Bonds entitle you to ________ for a fixed term if the business or government does not go bankrupt.
   A. revenues
   B. opportunity costs
   C. interest

3. MC: Lack of ________ allows bonds to pay a lower rate of return than stocks.
   A. profits
   B. volatility
   C. diversification

4. MC: Random walk theory suggests that:
   A. you can't make money in the stock market.
   B. only an expert can make money in the stock market.
   C. you can earn an average return from an index fund with less risk.

5. MC: The primary reason for switching from stocks to bonds when you will soon need the money is to:
   A. avoid having to sell stocks at temporarily low prices.
   B. protect against inflation.
   C. avoid the "random walk."

6. Risk refers to the ___________ of possible outcomes.
   A. danger
   B. variance
   C. liquidity

7. Diverse investments fluctuate:
   A. independently.
   B. predictably.
   C. primarily in the long-term.

8. Planning to beat the market may lead you to:
   A. put off investing.
   B. pick an index fund.
   C. invest in bonds.

Lecture 31

Managing Risk

Vocabulary

(Open book: Students should use the glossary at the back of the book, as well as a dictionary, to identify the correct answers. Format: matching)

Home equity	A specified amount of money that the insured must pay before an insurance company will pay a claim
Mortgage	The value of a homeowner's interest in their home; the real market value minus the amount owed on the mortgage
Deductible	A payment made by a beneficiary (especially for health services) in addition to that made by an insurer
Copay	An instrument used to borrow funds against an asset such as a house

Quiz

(Closed book)

1. MC: To avoid paying premiums for mortgage insurance, you need to pay ______% of the sale price in a down payment.
   A. 20
   B. 5
   C. 35

2. T/F: If a mortgage payment would be less than or equal to the rent you currently pay, you should buy a home instead.

3. How is education different from most other investments?
   A. You can take out loans to finance it.
   B. You don't get to choose how much money to invest in it.
   C. You have a lot more control over whether it turns out to have a good return.

4. MC: Average earning for college graduates varies greatly depending on:
    A. college major.
    B. stock market fluctuations.
    C. debt levels.

5. MC: If you prioritize other things above a college education:
    A. you probably should change your priorities.
    B. you probably should not pay for college.
    C. you probably should take out more student loans.

6. MC: How much should you work while in college?
    A. Until it starts crowding out higher-return uses of your time
    B. Enough to fully cover your tuition
    C. Not at all

7. MC: Insurance:
    A. spreads risk across a pool of individuals.
    B. increases risk.
    C. is always a good deal.

8. MC: Compared to renting, home-buying involves significant:
    A. risk-sharing.
    B. transaction costs.
    C. deductibles.

9. MC: You should select an insurance plan with:
    A. the best coverage.
    B. the best mix of coverage and risk based on your preferences.
    C. the lowest premiums.

10. T/F: The purpose of insurance is to pay for regular, certain occurrences.

Short Answer

1. What career are you interested in? Research the requirements and median pay at https://www.bls.gov/ooh/.

2. What were your medical expenses last year? Based on your general health and willingness to accept risk, should you get health insurance with more or less coverage?

Lecture 32

Conclusion

Vocabulary

(Open book: Students should use the glossary at the back of the book, as well as a dictionary, to identify the correct answers. Format: matching)

Incentives	The tendency of market prices to direct individuals pursuing their own self-interest into activities that pro-mote the economic well-being of the society
Scarcity	The study of decision-making as it affects the formation and operation of collective organizations such as governments. In general the principles and methodology of economies are applied to political science top-ics.
Opportunity cost	The change in total value or benefit derived from an action such as consumption of an additional unit of a good or service
Marginal benefit	The highest valued alternative good or activity that must be sacrificed as a result of choosing an option
Public choice analysis	Condition in which people would like to have more of a good or resources than is freely available from na-ture
Invisible hand	The expected payoffs from actions

Quiz

(Closed book)

1. MC: Catholic Social Teaching leaves it to decision-makers' judgment:
   - A. what goals to pursue.
   - B. how best to pursue its ideals.
   - C. how to convert people to Catholicism.

2. T/F: When the benefits are concentrated on a small group and the costs dispersed across a large number of people, policies can be adopted that are a net loss.

3. T/F: Economic thinking applies only to economic decisions.

4. MC: Scarcity forces us to make:
   A. bad choices.
   B. tradeoffs.
   C. money.

5. MC: As you have more of one thing, additional units tend to:
   A. be more and more valuable.
   B. be less and less valuable.
   C. stay the same value.

6. MC: The wealth of a nation is determined by:
   A. the number of jobs that are created.
   B. how much money is in circulation.
   C. its production of goods and services, and their allocation.

7. MC: Knowing the unintended consequences of fuel efficiency requirements:
   A. tells us that the requirements are bad policy.
   B. tells us the requirements are good policy.
   C. gives us information to weigh costs against benefits.

8. T/F: Economics can tell us when to value fairness more than economic growth.

9. T/F: Some things are too important to consider the costs involved.

10. MC: Economic thinking can help decision-makers identify the most effective way to uphold principles of Catholic Social Teaching because:
   A. economic thinking shows us that we should prioritize material well-being above all else.
   B. economic thinking shows that government officials always pursue the common good.
   C. economic thinking helps illuminate direct and indirect effects of choices.

Short answer

1. What is one principle of economic thinking that made an impression on you? How will understanding that change your decisions? Give one example of how you will apply it in your life.

2. What module was most interesting to you? Give an example of how it helped you understand the world or people's choices better.

Answer Key

Lecture 1

Vocabulary

Incentives: The expected payoffs from actions

Scarcity: Condition in which people would like to have more of a good or resources than is freely available from nature

Resource: An input used to produce economic goods and services. Natural resources, labor, skills, entrepreneurial talent, and capital are examples.

Allocate: Distribute for a particular purpose

Quiz

1. C
2. T
3. A
4. F
5. B
6. C
7. A
8. B
9. T
10. A

Short Answer

1. Full credit answers should draw from the book and lecture.
   Example: Someone decides; first-come, first-served; violence; prices. Prices are the most fair because the person who values the good the most will get it.

2. Full credit answers should explain that scarcity forces us to make tradeoffs with our choices.
   Example: Scarcity means we have fewer goods and resources than we'd like. That means we have to make choices about how to use those resources – every choice involves a tradeoff, because if we use a scarce resource for one use, there's less of that resource for other uses.

Lecture 2

Vocabulary

Incentives: The expected payoffs from actions

Monetary: Relating to money

Non-monetary: Not in the form of money

Capitalism: An economic system characterized by private or corporate ownership of capital goods, by investments that are determined by private decision, and by prices, production, and the distribution of goods that are determined mainly by competition in a free market

Socialism: An economic system characterized by collective or governmental ownership and administration of the means of production and distribution of goods

Input: A component of production (such as land, labor, or raw materials)

Altruistic: Having or showing an unselfish concern for the welfare of others

Postulate: A hypothesis advanced as an essential presupposition, condition, or premise of a train of reasoning

Materialistic: Overly concerned or preoccupied with material possessions rather than with intellectual or spiritual things

Market: An abstract concept that encompasses the trading arrangements of buyers and sellers that underlie the forces of supply and demand

Quiz

1. A
2. C
3. F
4. B
5. C
6. T
7. C
8. B
9. A
10. T

Short Answer

1. Full-credit answers should identify the costs and benefits of picking up the penny, and compare to the costs and benefits of picking up the quarter.
   Example: The cost in time and effort is the same, but the benefit of picking up the quarter is much higher.

2. Full-credit answers should discuss some things that would change the relative costs and benefits between the options, and how those changes in costs and benefits would affect your decision.
   Example: The higher the pay at the restaurant, the higher the benefit to working (and the higher the opportunity cost of choosing to spend the summer at the beach), so you'd be more likely to work at the restaurant. The more friends who are working over the summer, the lower the benefit of spending your time at the beach (and the lower the opportunity cost of working), so you'd be less likely to spend time at the beach.

3. Full-credit answers should discuss incentives and explain that all people are motivated to pursue their goals, whether or not those goals are selfish.
   Example: Everyone is self-interested. This means they respond to incentives, weighing the costs and benefits of their choices, including non-monetary costs and benefits. This doesn't mean they are selfish and care only about themselves. Being selfish means you only care about costs and benefits to yourself. Even people who consider the costs and benefits to others are responding to incentives.

4. Full-credit answers should include several items. The list in the example answer is not exhaustive.
   Example: Time, effort, health, safety, enjoyment, emotional impact, benefits and costs to others

Lecture 3

Vocabulary

Resource: An input used to produce economic goods and services. Natural resources, labor, skills, entrepreneurial talent, and capital are examples.

Scarcity: Condition in which people would like to have more of a good or resources than is freely available from nature

Opportunity cost: The highest valued alternative good or activity that must be sacrificed as a result of choosing an option

Forgo: Omit or decline to take (something pleasant or valuable); go without

Subsidy: A government payment or tax credit provided to either the producers or consumers of certain goods

Quiz

1. F
2. C
3. F
4. F
5. A
6. B
7. B
8. A
9. C
10. A

Short Answer

1. Full-credit answers should describe both scarcity and poverty and explain that even if everyone has their basic needs fulfilled, scarcity will always exist.
   Example: Poverty means not being able to fulfill one's basic needs. Only some people live in poverty, and many people escape poverty every day. Scarcity means we have limited resources to fulfill our unlimited wants. Everyone will always face scarcity. Even very wealthy people face scarcity: Their money is still finite, and they also face scarcity of other resources, such as time.

2. Full-credit answers should include a description of scarcity and give examples of some resources that will always be scarce.
   Example: Scarcity means we have limited resources to fulfill our unlimited wants. Resources that are limited include time and natural resources. Since these resources will always be limited, and by nature, human beings would always enjoy having more goods and services, our ability to produce goods and services will always fall short of our desire for those goods and services. That is, scarcity will always exist, and we will be forced to make tradeoffs.

3. Full-credit answers should include the idea of tradeoffs and opportunity cost.
   Example: Even if a lunch is provided to you free of charge, you still have an opportunity cost of consuming that lunch. The opportunity cost is the next-best thing you could have done with your time. You have to make a tradeoff of that alternative use of your time if you wish to take advantage of the "free" lunch, so it's not actually costless even if it has zero monetary cost.

4. Full-credit answers should be the next-best use of that $40 to you. Recall that opportunity cost is not *all* possible things you could purchase with $40, but just your next-highest-valued use of the $40. Thus, "A $40 dinner, $40 of gas, and a $40 pair of shoes" would be an *incorrect* answer.
   Example: The opportunity cost to me of purchasing a sweatshirt for $40 would be a concert ticket for $35 and a beverage for $5, as that would be my next-favorite use of $40.

Lecture 4

Vocabulary

Marginal: A term used to describe the effects of a change in the current situation; additional

Marginal benefit: The change in total value or benefit derived from an action such as consumption of an additional unit of a good or service

Marginal cost: The change in total cost resulting from an action such as the production of an additional unit of output

Diminishing: Decreasing, declining

Utility: Benefit or value

Quiz

1. C
2. B
3. B
4. B
5. B
6. T
7. C
8. C
9. A
10. F

Short Answer

1. Full-credit answers should identify that the cheapest per gallon is the whole gallon, but that does not mean you should necessarily buy the gallon.
   Example: The whole gallon is cheaper per gallon than the half-gallon, but that doesn't tell me whether I should buy the whole gallon. The marginal benefit of the whole over the half is a half a gallon more milk. The marginal cost of the whole over the half is $1. So I should buy the whole gallon only if an additional half-gallon is worth $1 or more to me.
2. Answers will vary.
3. Full-credit answers should explain that the marginal utility of a good differs based on how much has already been consumed.
   Example: The marginal utility of a good varies based on how much has already been consumed. If you had eaten nothing all day, one slice of bread would have high marginal utility, while the fifth slice of bread would have much lower marginal utility.

Lecture 5

Vocabulary

Value: The importance, worth, or usefulness of something

Allocate: Distribute for a particular purpose

Division of labor: A method that breaks down the production of a commodity into a series of specific tasks, each performed by a different worker

Specialization: The process of concentrating on and becoming expert in a particular subject or skill

Economies of scale: Reductions in the firm's per-unit costs that occur when large factories are used to produce large volumes of output

Law of comparative advantage: Individuals, firms, regions or nations can produce a larger output and achieve mutual gains from trade by specializing in the production of goods they can produce at low opportunity cost

Quiz

1. C
2. A
3. B
4. F
5. A
6. B
7. A
8. A
9. C
10. B

Short Answer

1. Full-credit answers should demonstrate understanding that a person has a comparative advantage in something if they have a lower opportunity cost of doing it.
   Example: If someone has the comparative advantage producing something, it means they have the lower opportunity cost of production.

2. Full-credit answers should reflect the idea that because people have different tastes and preferences, they will value the same good differently. Value, therefore, is subjective.
   Example: Everyone values things differently. For example, I prefer vanilla ice cream to chocolate ice cream, but some other people prefer chocolate to vanilla, and others don't care for ice cream at all. Vanilla ice cream has no fixed value, but brings different levels of enjoyment to different people.

3. A. Trade creates value by moving goods from people who value them less to people who value them more.
   B. Trade enables specialization, thereby making it possible to produce and consume more goods and services.
   C. Trade enables economies of scale, thereby lowering production costs.

Lecture 6

Vocabulary

Transaction costs: The time, effort, and other resources needed to search out, negotiate, and consummate an exchange of goods or services

Productive capacity: The maximum amount a country can produce given its inputs

Tariff: A tax on imports

Quota: A specific limit or maximum quantity or value of a good that is permitted to be imported into a country during a given period

Occupational licensing: A requirement that a person obtain permission from the government in order to perform certain business activities or work in certain occupations

Price controls: Prices that are imposed by the government. The prices may be set either above or below the level that would be established by markets.

Middlemen: People who buy and sell goods or services or arrange trades

Quiz

1. A
2. B
3. A
4. A
5. F
6. C
7. B
8. C
9. F
10. T

Short Answer

1. Full-credit answers should include three examples of professions or innovations that make transportation of products easier and cheaper, that make it easier and cheaper for buyers and sellers to find each other, or that make it easier and cheaper for buyers to know the quality and attributes of a product.
   Examples: Providing electronic rather than physical versions of things, such as ebooks; fax machines; semi-trucks; interstate highway systems; mail and package delivery; talent scouting; PayPal; ride-share apps; certifications of quality.
2. Full-credit answers should demonstrate understanding of the search costs involved in identifying the quality or attributes of a product.
   Example: Brands have a known reputation for a consistent level of quality and price point. This reduces search costs, as buyers know what to expect of a known brand's products without having to do a lot of research on a specific product.
3. Full-credit answers should demonstrate understanding that transactions costs, by reducing trade, also reduce the gains from trade.
   Example: Geographic barriers increase transportation costs. Higher transportation costs reduce trade, and thus reduce the gains from trade. Limiting the market to people nearby limits the efficiency gains of economies of scale and the ability of people to specialize in their comparative advantage.

Lecture 7

Vocabulary

Law of demand: As the price of something rises, people want to buy less of it. As the price falls, people want to buy more.

Demand: The quantity people want to buy at any given price. (Represented by a downward-sloping curve.)

Quantity demanded: The amount people want to buy at a particular price. (A single point on the demand curve.)

Law of supply: As the price of something rises, producers are willing to supply more. As the price falls, producers supply less.

Supply: The quantity people are willing to supply at any given price. (Represented by an upward-sloping curve.)

Quantity supplied: The amount that will be supplied at a particular price. (A single point on the supply curve.)

Cost of production: The opportunity cost of the inputs

Quiz

1. B
2. A
3. C
4. B
5. F
6. B
7. A
8. C
9. A
10. T

Short Answer

1.

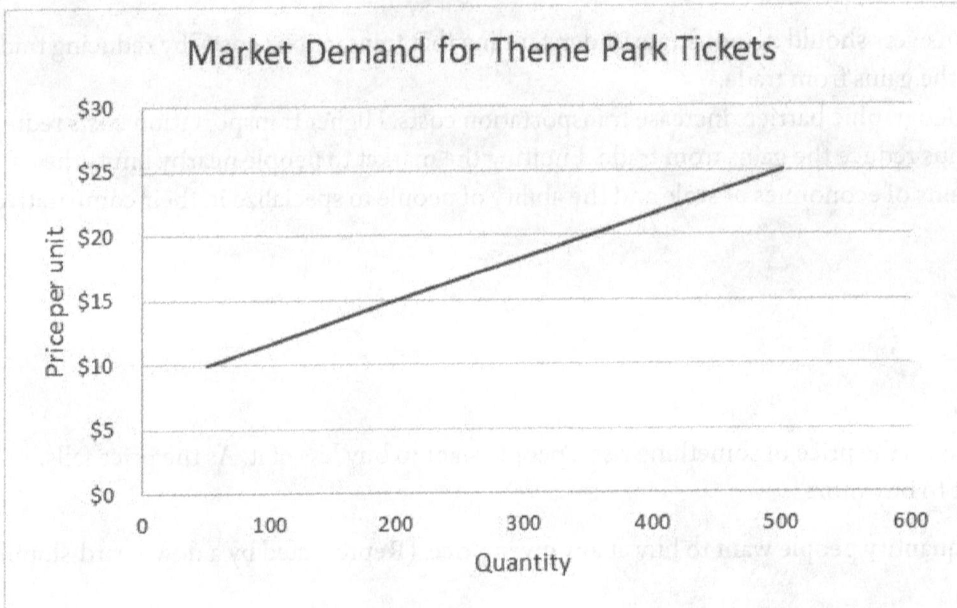

2. Between $20 and $25

3.

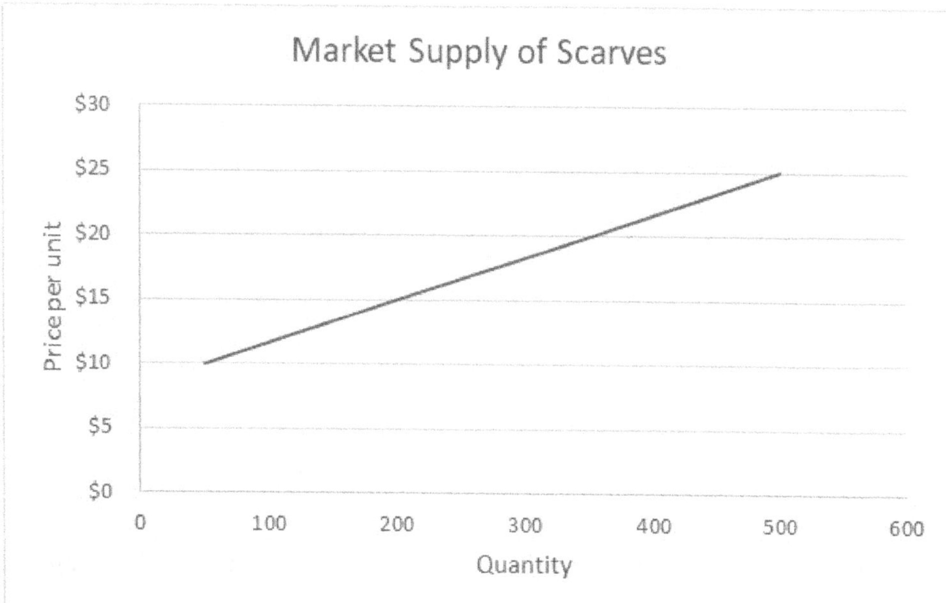

4. A. $15
   B. Between 350 and 500

6. Full-credit answers should be close to the definitions of demand and supply.
   Example: The demand curve represents the quantity of a good that a person or group is willing to buy at different prices. The supply curve represents the quantity of a good that will be produced and sold at different prices.

7. Full-credit answers should discuss diminishing marginal utility.
   Example: Demand curves slope downward because goods take on diminishing marginal utility. The shape of the demand curve reflects how much a change in price will affect the quantity demanded; this will be different for different products and at different quantities of those products.

Lecture 8

Vocabulary

Equilibrium: The price that brings supply and demand into balance

Economic efficiency: A condition in which all actions for which the benefits exceed the cost are taken, and no actions for which the cost exceeds the benefits are taken

Substitute goods: Products that serve similar purposes

Shortage: A condition in which the amount of a good offered for sale by producers is less than the amount demanded by buyers at the existing price

Surplus: A condition in which the amount of a good offered for sale by producers is greater than the amount that buyers will purchase at the existing price

Quiz

1. F
2. B
3. C
4. A
5. T
6. B
7. A
8. A
9. C
10. C

Short Answer

1. Full-credit answers should demonstrate understanding that the equilibrium price is the unique price where the quantity demanded is equal to the quantity supplied.
   Example: At prices lower than equilibrium, people are willing to buy more than sellers are willing to sell. In other words, buyers' marginal utility is higher than sellers' cost of production. At prices higher than the equilibrium price, sellers are willing to sell more than buyers are willing to buy. Put another way, buyers' marginal utility is lower than sellers' cost of production.

2. Full-credit answers should demonstrate understanding of how buyers and sellers naturally respond to shortages or surpluses.
   Example: At prices above equilibrium, sellers are motivated to lower their prices in order to avoid a surplus. At prices below equilibrium, buyers are motivated to bid up the price.

3. Full-credit answers should highlight the difference between the demand curve and a single point on the demand curve.
   Example: Demand is how many units people are willing to buy at any given price. It is graphically represented by a curve. Quantity demanded is the amount people are willing to buy at a particular price. It is represented by a single point along the demand curve.

4. Full-credit answers should include examples of factors that change how much buyers are willing to buy at any given price.
   Example: Answers will vary but students should include several of the following in their answer: a change in incomes, a broad change in tastes or preferences (e.g., for healthier food), a change in the price of substitute goods, a change in population.

5. Full-credit answers should demonstrate understanding of buyers demanding more of a substitute good, increasing the equilibrium price in that market.
   Example: Higher prices for a particular product will induce buyers to shift to substitutes, thereby increasing the demand for those substitute goods. An increase in demand will lead to a higher equilibrium price for the substitute. At the same time, producers will be incentivized to produce more of the original good, so they will increase their demand for inputs, thereby increasing the equilibrium prices of those inputs.

Lecture 9

Vocabulary

Profit: The amount by which total revenue exceeds total cost

Cost: The opportunity cost of inputs

Loss: The amount by which sales revenue fails to cover the cost of supplying a good or service

Entrepreneur: Someone who takes risks and brings new products or services to the market

Capital: Buildings, tools, machinery and other equipment used in production

Revenue: Price of all goods sold times quantity of goods sold

Quiz

1. A
2. T
3. A
4. B
5. B
6. B
7. T
8. C
9. T
10. A

Short Answer

1. Full-credit answers should include a discussion of supply and demand, as well as opportunity cost of the inputs.
   Example: The cost of inputs is determined by the supply and demand for those resources. The cost of inputs reflects the opportunity cost of those resources.

2. Full-credit answers should discuss the role of entrepreneurs, and the information that profits and losses convey to producers.
   Example: Entrepreneurs take on projects they expect to be profitable; that is, they expect the inputs they buy can be put to more valuable use than the alternatives. When that expectation turns out to be wrong, and consumers don't want to buy their product at a price that covers their costs, the entrepreneurs lose money and will eventually go out of that business.

3. Full-credit answers should discuss the highest-valued use of a resource.
   Example: Efficient allocation of resources means those resources are put to their highest valued use.

Lecture 10

Vocabulary

Value: The importance, worth, or usefulness of something

Economic efficiency: A condition in which all actions for which the benefits exceed the cost are taken, and no actions for which the cost exceeds the benefits are taken

Entrepreneur: Someone who takes risks and brings new products or services to the market

Non-monetary: Not in the form of money

Quiz

1. B
2. C
3. F
4. B
5. A
6. C
7. A
8. A
9. F
10. T

Short Answer

1. Full-credit answers should offer some suggestions, as well as presenting the costs and benefits of pursuing a high income.
   Example: To pursue a higher income, you can build skills through education or training, work long hours, do well at your job to build an impressive resume, be willing to move, and make other sacrifices in return for income.
   Costs could include the next-best alternative uses of your time, being away from family, stress, and the next-best alternative use of money spent on education. The benefits of a high income are the ability to purchase a wide variety of goods and services and the ability to save more for the future.
2. Full-credit answers should draw from the lecture.
   Example: Flexible hours, pleasant work environment, prestige, a sense of purpose, feeling of community, generous time off.

3. Full-credit answers should explain the marginal utility of each job and the relationship between marginal utility and salary.
   Example: Because even though the work teachers do is valuable, there are far more teachers than movie stars. The marginal utility of each individual teacher is relatively low compared to that of a movie star. Salaries reflect the marginal utility rather than average utility of a type of worker.

Lecture 11

Vocabulary

Invisible Hand: The tendency of market prices to direct individuals pursuing their own self-interest into activities that promote the economic well-being of the society.

Capitalism: An economic system characterized by private or corporate ownership of capital goods, by investments that are determined by private decision, and by prices, production, and the distribution of goods that are determined mainly by competition in a free market

Socialism: An economic system characterized by collective or governmental ownership and administration of the means of production and distribution of goods

Market: An abstract concept that encompasses the trading arrangements of buyers and sellers that underlie the forces of supply and demand

Quiz

1. C
2. A
3. T
4. A
5. C
6. B
7. C
8. B
9. T
10. C

Short Answer

1. Full-credit answers should explain the relationship of price to consumers' value and the opportunity cost of inputs, and what incentives prices create for buyers and sellers.
   Example: Market prices register the choices of millions of consumers, producers, and resource suppliers. They reflect information about consumer preferences and costs. Changing prices give consumers the incentive to buy more or less of a product. Through profits and losses, prices give producers the incentive to avoid high-opportunity-cost inputs and seek low-cost production methods.
2. Full-credit answers should explain the difference between central planning and a price system, and how information is communicated and coordinated in each system.
   Example: Market prices contain all the information needed to bring demand and supply into harmony. They direct producers and resource suppliers toward production of those things that consumers value most, relative to their cost. Without price signals, no central authority could possibly acquire all the information needed to coordinate economic activity efficiently—that is, channeling goods and resources to their highest-valued use.
3. Full-credit answers should list at least some of the following.
   Example: A free-market is also called: laissez faire, price system, and capitalism; central planning is also called: communism, socialism, authoritarianism.

Lecture 12

Vocabulary

Great Depression: The longest and most severe economic downturn in modern history, lasting throughout the 1930s

Secondary effects: Consequences of a change that are not immediately identifiable but are felt only with the passage of time

Mandate: An official order or command

Tariffs: A tax on goods imported into a country

Import quota: A specific limit or maximum quantity or value of a good that is permitted to be imported into a country during a given period

Public policy: A course of action undertaken by the government with the aim of achieving a particular goal

Quiz

1. B
2. B
3. C
4. C
5. A
6. A
7. A
8. B
9. A
10. T

Short Answer

1. Full-credit answers should mention secondary effects or unintended consequences.
   Example: The broken window fallacy ignores the secondary effects.

2. Full-credit answers should identify that first-order effects are direct effects, and second-order effects are indirect effects.
   Example: A first-order effect is the direct, short-term, and easily seen result of an action or policy. A second-order, or indirect, effect is often unseen or longer-term, and can be intended or unintended.

3. Full-credit answers should discuss the unforeseen nature of both the invisible hand and some indirect effects.
   Example: Both involve cause-and-effect, specifically indirect effects. Both involve effects that were not part of the intention of the decision-maker. The invisible hand involves coordination of more information than any human mind could possibly possess; unintended consequences covered in this chapter, by contrast, could be foreseen if we thought about it clearly enough.

Lecture 13

Vocabulary

Living standard: Material well-being

Extreme or absolute poverty: Defined by the World Bank as living on less than $1.90 per day

Gross domestic product (GDP): The market value of all goods and services in their final (rather than intermediate) use that are produced within a country during a specific period. It is a measure of both income and output.

GDP per capita: A country's economic output per person

Economic prosperity: Persistent increases in per capita income and improvements in the standard of living

Quiz

1. B
2. F
3. A
4. B
5. B
6. A
7. C
8. F
9. B
10. C

Short Answer

1. Full-credit answers should include not only material goods but also immaterial factors contributing to well-being.
   Example: Health, education, recreation opportunities, cheap access to abundant clean water, more product variety, more ability to afford necessities and luxury goods.
2. Full-credit answers should discuss the opportunity cost of using enormous quantities of labor for low-productivity purposes.
   Example: Using hand tools requires much more labor, making the dam far more expensive to build. This means that it diverts resources and labor away from more productive uses. Inefficient production decreases the overall productivity and wealth of an economy, making people worse off.
3. Full-credit answers should identify that existing producers in that industry gain while the reduction in production decreases GDP and overall wealth.
   Example: Producers in that particular industry are helped, because the reduction in supply causes the equilibrium price of the goods they produce to increase. The general public is worse off because they have to spend more for that product and thus have less to spend on other things.
4. Full-credit answers should discuss the difference between material and spiritual well-being.
   Example: He defined it as ignoring the existence of goods which by their nature are not and cannot be mere commodities. In other words, caring only about material well-being, and ignoring spiritual and emotional needs.

Lecture 14

Vocabulary

Physical capital: Human-made resources such as tools, equipment, and structures

Human capital: The abilities, skills, and health of human beings that contribute to the production of both current and future output

Economic rules (economic organization): The public policies that govern the economy

Economic growth (economic progress): An increase in the production of goods and services in an economy

Investment: The purchase, construction, or development of capital resources, including both non-human and human capital

Quiz

1. B
2. C
3. T
4. A
5. A
6. B
7. T
8. A
9. B
10. C

Short Answer

Full-credit answers should draw on the book and lecture.
Example: Decreasing the cost of production; decreasing transaction costs; and introducing beneficial products and services to consumers

Full-credit answers should relate entrepreneurship to innovation.
Example: Creative entrepreneurs figure out better ways to use our existing resources. By taking risks on new ideas and innovations, they improve our technology, expand the array of goods and services for consumers, and decrease the cost and increase the quality of available goods and services.

Full-credit answers should draw on the book and lecture.
Example: Investments in physical and human capital; improvements in technology; improvements in economic organization (economic rules)

Lecture 15

Vocabulary

Private property rights: The rights to exclusive use, legal protection against invaders, and the right to transfer to others

Productivity: The average output produced per worker during a specific time period, usually measured as output per hour worked

Rule of law: The authority and influence of law in society; the principle whereby all members of a society (including those in government) are considered equally subject to publicly disclosed legal codes and processes.

Public policy: A course of action undertaken by the government with the aim of achieving a particular goal

Quiz

1. B
2. B
3. A
4. A
5. B
6. C
7. C
8. B
9. A
10. T

Short Answer

1. Full-credit answers should draw on the book and lecture.
   Example: By protecting private property rights, enforcing contracts, and upholding the rule of law.

2. Full-credit answers should draw on the book and lecture.
   Example: Incentives under private ownership:

   A. maintain and care for items they own,
   B. use and develop their property in ways others value highly,
   C. prevent damages from use of their property,
   D. conserve resources for the future.

9. If your employer offers to match your investment, you should probably:
   A. reject it as too good to be true.
   B. invest at least to the maximum match.
   C. invest just enough for a rainy day.

10. T/F: You should always invest in bonds, as they are less risky than stocks.

Short Answer

1. Why is it a bad idea to believe you can "beat the market" with your stock portfolio?
2. What are some situations when you will want to switch stocks for bonds?
3. How can you diversify your investments?

3. Answers will vary.
   Example:

    A. Owners of generators have the incentive to ensure the machinery is properly taken care of so it will work well and last a long time.
    B. Owners of book copyrights have the incentive to sell the film rights to interested movie studios.
    C. Owners of theme parks have the incentive to ensure patrons will not be injured on rides.
    D. Owners of geese that lay golden eggs have the incentive not to kill the goose.

4. Full-credit answers should explain how a person can recoup long-term investments by selling.
   Example: The market value of the property at any point in time will reflect the expected future value of the resources included in the property.

Lecture 16

Vocabulary

Innovation: A new method, product, or idea

Investor: Someone who provides a business with capital, with the expectation of a future financial gain

Entrepreneur: Someone who takes risks and brings new products or services to the market

Capitalism: An economic system characterized by private or corporate ownership of capital goods, by investments that are determined by private decision, and by prices, production, and the distribution of goods that are determined mainly by competition in a free market

Quiz

1. C
2. C
3. F
4. B
5. A
6. C
7. B
8. A
9. C
10. T

Short Answer

1. Full-credit answers should discuss the importance for developers to be able to recoup upfront costs.
   Example: Initial purchasers make it worthwhile to create new products in the first place, covering the high upfront costs of developing the product. Sellers generally find ways to improve the quality and lower the price over the years, allowing later customers to benefit from what was, effectively, funded by early adopters.
2. Full-credit answers should discuss the varying importance of economies of scale.
   Example: In some sectors, economies of scale are of great importance. Investing in factories or other mass production processes that cut per-unit cost only makes sense if you can recoup this investment by selling a lot of units. Other sectors rely on local connections or knowledge, or workers who have developed a particular skill, and cannot operate as efficiently if they are too big.
3. Full-credit answers should discuss competition and willingness to pay.
   Example: Buyers compete by bidding for products they value—those willing to pay a higher price are able to buy the good. Sellers compete to offer the products consumers value at the lowest price. In order to succeed, they must discover efficient production methods with low opportunity cost.
4. Answers will vary.
   Example: Quality of product, service, location, and convenience.

Lecture 17

Vocabulary

Monopoly: A market characterized by a single seller of a well-defined product for which there are no good substitutes; and high barriers to the entry of any other firms into the market for that product

Oligopoly: A state of limited competition, in which a market is shared by a small number of producers or sellers

Discretion: The power or right to decide or act according to one's own judgment

Lucrative: Highly profitable

Proponent: Advocate, supporter

Certification: Confirms the education, training, and other qualifications of an individual, but does not prohibit noncertified individuals from competing in the market

Occupational licensing: A requirement that a person obtain permission from the government in order to perform certain business activities or work in certain occupations

Quiz

1. B
2. C
3. A
4. A
5. B
6. A
7. C
8. F
9. T
10. C

Short Answer

1. Full-credit answers should draw on the book and lecture.
   Example: Restricting sellers from entering a market, undermining the evenly applied rule of law, and preventing prices from adjusting freely.

2. Full-credit answers should discuss competition.
   Example: Such regulations protect existing sellers from competition, so they don't have to try as hard to keep improving their products and lowering their costs.

3. Full-credit answers should draw on the book and lecture.
   Example: Price floors keep the price above equilibrium, creating excess supply of the product. Price ceilings keep the price below equilibrium, creating a shortage of the product. The price controls keep the market from adjusting to the price that brings quantity supplied and demanded into balance.

4. Full-credit answers should distinguish rule of law from discretionary decision-making.
   Example: If government officials have the power to decide who must comply with regulations, that means they can make their decisions at their own discretion instead of the law applying equally to everyone. Favoritism and bribery are likely outcomes.

5. Full-credit answers should identify that a minimum wage is a price floor, which will result in excess supply, or surplus, of labor.
   Example: By setting a price floor, a minimum wage creates an excess supply of workers. (More people want jobs at the minimum wage than employers are willing to offer.) Positive effects: Those who keep their jobs will have a higher income. Negative effects: There is reduced employment of low-skilled workers; reduced hours worked and fewer fringe benefits for workers who keep their jobs; increased prices of products impacted by the higher minimum wage (e.g., fast food); and young workers are prevented from acquiring experience and skills that could help them move up the employment ladder.

6. Full-credit answers should draw on the book.
   Example: Most minimum-wage workers are members of households with incomes above the poverty level; low-income consumers will be harder hit by price increases from businesses passing on higher costs due to the minimum wage; and the majority of low-income households in the US do not have anyone in the labor force

Lecture 18

Vocabulary

Capital investment: Expenditure on buildings, machinery, tools, and other equipment that will enhance future productivity
Investment goods or capital goods: Goods or facilities bought or constructed for the purpose of producing future economic benefits
Consumer goods: Goods produced for present use
Saving: A reduction in current consumption in order to make the funds available for other uses
Capital market: The markets for stocks, bonds, and real estate
Crony capitalism: A situation in which the allocation of resources and capital is substantially influenced by political decision-making rather than by market forces

Quiz

1. B
2. A
3. C
4. A
5. B
6. F
7. B
8. T
9. B
10. C

Short Answer

1. Full-credit answers should draw on the book and lecture.
   Example: Capital enables more efficient production through use of machinery, increasing economic output. By allowing entrepreneurs to produce their inventions, it improves technology, which also improves living standards.

2. Full-credit answers should explain the relationship of risk and interest rates charged in a private market, and the goal of these lending enterprises to reduce interest rates for high-risk buyers.
   Example: They provided more loans to higher-risk borrowers and at a lower interest rate than the private market would have offered to high-risk borrowers. They separated the interest rate from the riskiness of the investment.

Lecture 19

Vocabulary

Money: Anything that is generally accepted as final payment for goods and services by buyers and sellers

Money supply: The supply of currency and checking account funds in a country

Medium of exchange: Any item that is widely acceptable in exchange for goods and services

Monetary policy: The deliberate control of the national money supply and, in some cases, credit conditions, by the government

Inflation: A general increase in the price level

Unit of account: A measure of value in terms of which accounts are kept and values stated

Fiat currency: A form of money issued by a government and declared to be legal tender. This type of currency is not linked to any asset of value and can be printed at will by central governments.

Quiz

1. B
2. T
3. C
4. A
5. T
6. B
7. C
8. A
9. A
10. B

Short Answer

1. Full-credit answers should draw on the book and lecture.
   Example: Store of value (allows people to hold value they have traded for until they want to exchange again); medium of exchange (lowers transaction costs, making more trades possible); unit of account (standard of common value all goods and services can be converted to).

2. Full-credit answers should draw on the book and lecture.
   Example:
   A. Durability: Shells can be fragile but are probably more durable than books, which could easily fall apart
   B. Portability: Shells are lighter and smaller than books
   C. Divisibility: Shells can be removed from a string and given to another, whereas books would be ruined by being taken apart
   D. Uniformity: Both shells and books could be reasonably uniform
   E. Stability: The availability of shells is more fixed than that of books, which can be created using a printing press
   F. Acceptability: This would depend on the society
3. Full-credit answers should explain inflation.
   Example: This causes inflation, or a general increase in prices. The instability of the currency will disrupt economic growth by discouraging saving and investing and reducing trade.
4. Full-credit answers should discuss the impact of inflation on investment and returns.
   Example: The resulting uncertainty makes capital investment projects more risky and less attractive. Thus, potential gains from trade, business activities, and capital formation will be lost.

Lecture 20

Vocabulary

Progressive income taxes: A tax in which the tax rate increases as the taxable amount increases

Marginal tax rate: The tax rate incurred on each additional dollar of income

Disincentive: A factor that discourages people from doing something

Perverse incentive: An incentive that has an unintended and undesirable result that is contrary to the intentions of its designers. A type of negative unintended consequence.

Free ride: A situation in which someone benefits without having to make a fair contribution

Quiz

1. A
2. C
3. F
4. F
5. A
6. B
7. B

8. 10% bracket: 10% of $9,875=$988
   12% bracket: 12% of $30,250=$3,630
   22% bracket: 22% of $45,399=$9,988
9. $1,074
10. Total tax: $15,680
    Average tax rate: $15,680/$90,000=17.42%
    Marginal tax rate: 24%

Short Answer

1. Full-credit answers should link income earned and value added, and explain how marginal tax rates reduce the benefits of earning a higher income.
   Example: Higher marginal tax rates reduce the benefits of undertaking costly actions required to pursue a higher income. These costly actions, such as seeking more education and training, would increase an individual's ability to provide value to others.
2. Full-credit answers should draw on the book and lecture.
   Example: People work fewer hours, invest less, purchase fewer goods, and spend more resources trying to avoid taxes.
3. Full-credit answers should mention government policies that may be considered beneficial.
   Example: There are things people would not voluntarily contribute enough to on their own, due to the ability to free-ride; there are things we want everyone to have the same level of access to regardless of income; and there are social safety net policies that can help people when private charity is insufficient.

Lecture 21

Vocabulary

Exchange rate: The rate at which one currency will be exchanged for another; also, the value of one country's currency in relation to another currency

Subsidiarity: A principle of social organization that holds that social and political issues should be dealt with at the most immediate (or local) level that is consistent with their resolution

Solidarity: Mutual support and care among people; a commitment to the common good

Specialization: The process of concentrating on and becoming expert in a particular subject or skill

Economies of scale: Reductions in the firm's per-unit costs that occur when large factories are used to produce large volumes of output

Law of comparative advantage: Individuals, firms, regions or nations can produce a larger output and achieve mutual gains from trade by specializing in the production of goods they can produce at low opportunity cost

Quiz

1. A
2. T
3. C
4. B
5. F
6. A
7. C
8. A
9. B
10. F

Short Answer

1. Full-credit answers should draw on the book and lecture.
   Example: People can acquire a good or service more cheaply from abroad than producing domestically; businesses can take advantage of economies of scale; increased trade promotes competition.

2. Full-credit answers should draw on the book and lecture.
   Example: High income countries disproportionately import goods made with low-income, low-skilled labor, and export goods requiring high-skilled labor. This reduces domestic demand for low-skill workers' labor. With access to global markets, less-developed countries like China and India have grown more rapidly than high-income developed nations.

3. Full-credit answers should draw on the book and lecture.
   Example: With international trade, countries can specialize in things they can do more efficiently, giving everyone access to more abundant and less expensive goods.

4. Full-credit answers should draw on the book and lecture.
   Example: Human dignity of all people, subsidiarity, solidarity

Lecture 22

Vocabulary

Economic efficiency: A situation in which all activities generating more benefit than cost are undertaken and no activities are undertaken for which the cost exceeds the benefit

Authoritarian regime: Any political system that concentrates power in the hands of a leader or a small elite that is not constitutionally responsible to the body of the people.

Autonomy: Independence or freedom; the right of self-government

Welfare state: A system whereby the government undertakes to protect the health and well-being of its citizens, especially those in financial or social need, by means of grants, pensions, and other benefits

Economic rules (economic organization): The public policies that govern the economy

Public choice analysis: The study of decision-making as it affects the formation and operation of collective organizations such as governments. In general the principles and methodology of economies are applied to political science topics.

Quiz

1. B
2. F
3. A
4. C
5. A
6. F
7. B
8. B
9. A
10. T

Short Answer

1. Full-credit answers should explain how government determines the economic rules.
   Example: Governments set rules determining what economic activity is allowed. They may also set rules affecting the incentives people face in the economy. Also, authoritarian regimes tend to have less free markets than do democracies.
2. Full-credit answers should explain solidarity and what kinds of policies would uphold solidarity.
   Example: Solidarity requires governments to defend the weak, limit employers' ability to set working conditions, and support the unemployed.

Lecture 23

Vocabulary

Barriers to entry: Obstacles that make it difficult for new companies to enter a given market, e.g. high fixed costs, government regulations, or patents

Merger: A combination of two or more companies into one larger company

Collusion: An agreement between firms that usually compete against each other to set the prices for their goods in order to gain an advantage

Market power: A company's ability to manipulate the price of an item in the marketplace by manipulating the level of supply

Public goods: Goods that are a) jointly consumed and b) nonexcludable

Externalities: Spillover effects that impose a cost or benefit on those who are not involved in the transaction

Quiz

1. B
2. C
3. T
4. C
5. F
6. A
7. A
8. B
9. A
10. C

Short Answer

1. Full-credit answers should draw on the book and lecture.
   Example: Ensuring a good environment for economic activity; supporting competition in the economy; and providing public goods
2. Full-credit answers should draw on the book and lecture.
   Example: Public goods and externalities
3. Full-credit answers should draw on the book and lecture.
   Example: Strong economies of scale, and government preventing competitors from entering a market

4. Full-credit answers should explain how government can increase positive externalities and decrease negative externalities.
   Example: In the case of negative externalities, government can tax the activity or set limits on production that generates negative externalities. In the case of positive externalities, government can subsidize the activity that generates positive externalities. The existence of positive externalities means the market may provide less than the optimal amount.

Lecture 24

Vocabulary

Dispersed: Spread out or distributed broadly

Special interest group: An organization of people united by a common interest

Lobbying: Lawfully seeking to influence the actions, policies, or decisions of government officials

Logrolling: The exchange between politicians of political support on one issue for political support on another

Rational ignorance: Choosing to be uninformed about an issue because the cost of becoming informed is greater than the potential benefit

Rent seeking: Trying to increase one's share of existing wealth without creating new wealth; attempts by individuals or groups to influence public policy to redistribute more income to themselves

Quiz

1. A
2. B
3. C
4. B
5. C
6. T
7. B
8. A
9. T
10. C

Short Answer

1. Full-credit answers should draw on the book and lecture.
   Example: Who benefits? Who pays? Who chooses?

2. Full-credit answers should identify who benefits, who pays, and who chooses in each scenario, and the incentives that creates.
   Example: In a free market, the answer to all those questions is generally the same. Everyone weighs his own costs and benefits—the incentives are aligned for efficient choices. In government, policymakers choose, while some of the general public benefit and others pay. This separation means the incentives are not aligned to promote efficient choices.

3. Full-credit answers should give the costs and benefits of being informed.
   Example: Being informed is costly and of little benefit in terms of affecting political outcomes, as an individual voter will virtually never decide the outcome of an election.

4. Full-credit answers should explain the incentives of politicians to create policies that have concentrated benefits and dispersed costs.
   Example: Politicians pursue specific groups of donors and voters by advancing policies that are strongly in the interests of those groups, at the expense of a majority of voters, who each are affected only very slightly by the policy.

5. Full-credit answers should explain the importance of low-interest borrowing for governments and how default would affect that.
   Example: Interest rates on debt will increase as investors fear default, and government may eventually actually default. This would disrupt the ability of the government to continue to function.

Lecture 25

Vocabulary

Command and control: An economic system in which government central planners control the means of production and determine the distribution of output

Common pool resource: A resource that benefits a group of people, but which provides diminished benefits to everyone if each individual pursues his or her own self-interest

Industrial policy: Organized government involvement in guiding the economy by encouraging investment in targeted industries

Decentralized: Controlled by state and local authorities rather than by the federal government

Quiz

1. C
2. A
3. B
4. A
5. A
6. T

7. A
8. B
9. F
10. A

Short Answer

1. Full-credit answers should explain why the information required is too extensive for effective central planning.
   Example: The equation central planners would need to solve involves knowing how much utility every individual would get from every marginal unit of every single good. Through prices, individuals convey information about their value and costs. These are constantly changing, and the information is uniquely known to each individual. This information would be impossible to convey directly to another decision-maker.

2. Full-credit answers should refer to the quotation at the beginning of page 150 in the book.
   Example: People have their own principle of motion, independent of the goals of the person seeking to arrange their movements.

3. Full-credit answers should explain how the political incentives may be at odds with creating a fair "middle way" system.
   Example: The poor and marginalized are least likely to have influence in politics. Unless there are strong limits on favoritism and lobbying by special interest groups, the incentives will tend to lead to policies benefiting the already wealthy and well-connected. Also, even well-intended policies to increase equality may have the unintended consequence of moving toward inefficient central planning, which would reduce economic progress for all.

Lecture 26

Vocabulary

Risk: The odds of losing money on an investment

Return: A measure of the profit or loss of an investment over time as a percentage of the original investment

Mortgage: A legal agreement by which a creditor lends money at interest in exchange for taking title of the debtor's property until the debt is repaid

Real interest rate: The interest rate adjusted for inflation; it indicates the real cost to the borrower (and yield to the lender) in terms of goods and services

Quiz

1. B
2. A
3. A
4. C
5. B
6. C
7. A
8. F
9. F
10. T

Short Answer

1. Full-credit answers should draw on the book and the lecture.
   Example: Debt allows you to do something that creates value, or produces value for you, sooner than you otherwise could.
2. Full-credit answers should identify the next best alternative use of the money.
   Example: The return you could get from investing that money.
3. Full-credit answers should explain that a plan is necessary to make good financial choices.
   Example: You can't avoid making financial choices: Avoiding making financial plans is a choice itself.

Lecture 27

Vocabulary

Value: The importance, worth, or usefulness of something

Economic efficiency: A condition in which all actions for which the benefits exceed the cost are taken, and no actions for which the cost exceeds the benefits are taken

Entrepreneur: Someone who takes risks and brings new products or services to the market

Non-monetary: Not in the form of money

Quiz

1. A
2. C
3. B
4. B
5. C

6. A
7. F
8. F
9. B
10. C

Short Answer

1. Full-credit answers should draw on the book and lecture.
   Example: Notice additional areas you can contribute; develop a portfolio of projects; earn a good reputation

2. Full-credit answers should explain comparative advantage.
   Example: Even if you think you are good at everything, there is some specialty that you have a comparative advantage in, and you will be better off focusing on that and hiring others to do other things. For example, professional weight-lifters would probably be great at moving boxes and furniture, but they are better off hiring a moving company and instead focusing their time on training and competitions. Likewise, even if you think you are worse at everything than others, there is still something you are relatively better at, and can gain from specializing in that and trading for other things.

Lecture 28

Vocabulary

Budget: Estimated income and itemized planned expenditures for a time period

Finance: To obtain money for, often through borrowing

Liquid asset: An asset that can be easily and quickly converted to purchasing power without loss of value

Credit: The ability of a customer to obtain goods or services before payment, based on the trust that payment will be made in the future

Quiz

1. C
2. C
3. B
4. B
5. A
6. B
7. A
8. F
9. T
10. T

Short Answer

1. Full-credit answers should discuss how a budget helps you acknowledge your spending habits. **Example:** A budget helps you channel resources to high-valued uses by forcing you to consider tradeoffs and opportunity costs. Increased spending in one area translates into decreased spending in another.

2. Full-credit answers should mention the importance of adjusting a budget to reflect priorities, as well as the importance of recognizing what is feasible to accomplish with a certain income. **Example:** Budgeting should be empowering. If I spend more in a category than I'd originally budgeted, then I have choices I can make: Reduce spending in another category, reduce spending in this category, or make more money. Budgeting helps me realize what's realistic given my income, as well as what's truly most important to me to spend on. This makes me feel better than continually spending more than I make but not having a specific plan for fixing that.

Lecture 29

Vocabulary

Interest: Money paid at a particular rate for the use of money lent

Compound interest: Interest that is earned not only on the principal but also on the interest previously earned

Principal: The original amount invested or lent

Rate of return: The profit from an investment, as a percentage of the original amount invested

Liquid asset: An asset that can be easily and quickly converted to purchasing power without loss of value

Certificate of Deposit (CD): A product offered by banks and credit unions that provides an interest rate premium in exchange for the customer agreeing to leave a lump-sum deposit untouched for a predetermined period of time.

Standard and Poor's (S&P) 500 index: A basket of five hundred stocks that are selected because they are thought to be collectively representative of the stock market as a whole

Quiz

1. B
2. B
3. A
4. A
5. C
6. F
7. A
8. F
9. F
10. C

Short Answer

1. Full credit answers should explain the importance of weighing the interest rate against the expected return of an investment.
   Example: If the interest on the loan exceeds your expected rate of return on investing the money, you should pay off the loan. Otherwise, it is costing you less than you are earning with the money.

2. Full credit answers should discuss compound interest and opportunity cost.
   Example: The reason to begin earlier is to take advantage of compound interest, which causes the money to grow vastly over time. Even with compound interest, however, it may make sense to put off saving if investing would have too high an opportunity cost: For example, if saving more would cause you to take out high-interest debt, or prevent you from investing in education or other investments that you expect will increase your income later on, or if you simply will get higher utility from spending the money now than from spending more money later on.

Lecture 30

Vocabulary

Stock: Ownership shares of a corporation

Bond: A promise to repay the principal (amount borrowed) plus interest at a specified time in the future

Principal: The amount of funds borrowed

Equities: Shares of stock in a company

Diversification: The strategy of investing in a number of diverse firms, industries, and instruments such as stocks, bonds, and real estate in order to minimize the risk accompanying investments

Portfolio: The holdings of savings, investments, and real assets such as real estate owned by an individual or financial institution

Mutual fund: An entity that pools the funds of investors and channels them into various categories of investments

Managed equity mutual fund: An equity mutual fund that has a portfolio manager who decides what stocks will be held in the fund and when they will be bought or sold

Indexed equity mutual fund: An equity mutual fund that holds a portfolio of stocks that matches their share (or weight) in a broad stock market index such as the S&P 500.

Random walk theory: The theory that current stock prices already reflect all known information about the future.

Quiz

1. B
2. C
3. B
4. C
5. A
6. B
7. A
8. A
9. B
10. F

Short Answer

1. Full-credit answers should draw on the book and lecture.
   Example: You are likely to put off investing at all until you have time to do market research, which means you will lose out on market gains in the meantime. You are likely to do worse with your investment than if you'd invested in an index fund. You are likely to put too much confidence in recommendations or "stock tips" from people who have made lucky guesses so far.
2. Full-credit answers should draw on the book and lecture.
   Example: When you will soon need the money for retirement, buying a home or paying for a child's education.
3. Full-credit answers should draw on the book and lecture.
   Example: By investing in a number of diverse firms, industries, and instruments such as stocks, bonds, and real estate in order to minimize the risk accompanying investments.

Lecture 31

Vocabulary

Home equity: The value of a homeowner's interest in their home; the real market value minus the amount owed on the mortgage

Mortgage: An instrument used to borrow funds against an asset such as a house

Deductible: A specified amount of money that the insured must pay before an insurance company will pay a claim

Copay: A payment made by a beneficiary (especially for health services) in addition to that made by an insurer

Quiz

1. A
2. F
3. C
4. A
5. B
6. A
7. A
8. B
9. B
10. F

Short Answer

1. Answers will vary.
   Example: According to the website, "Typically, postsecondary teachers must have a Ph.D. However, a master's degree may be enough for some postsecondary teachers at community colleges, and others may need work experience in their field of expertise." The median pay for postsecondary teachers is $79,540 per year.

2. Answers will vary.
   Example: My medical expenses last year were $1,000 for routine check-ups. I am fairly confident that my general good health will continue, and I'm willing to accept the risk that I may have high medical spending in the upcoming year and thus higher out-of-pocket expenses before the insurance kicks in. Thus, I should get insurance with less coverage and lower premiums.

Lecture 32

Vocabulary

Incentives: The expected payoffs from actions

Scarcity: Condition in which people would like to have more of a good or resources than is freely available from nature

Opportunity cost: The highest valued alternative good or activity that must be sacrificed as a result of choosing an option

Marginal benefit: The change in total value or benefit derived from an action such as consumption of an additional unit of a good or service

Public choice analysis: The study of decision-making as it affects the formation and operation of collective organizations such as governments. In general the principles and methodology of economies are applied to political science topics.

Invisible hand: The tendency of market prices to direct individuals pursuing their own self-interest into activities that promote the economic well-being of the society.

Quiz

1. B
2. T
3. F
4. B
5. B
6. C
7. C
8. F

9. F
10. C

Short Answer

1. Full-credit answers should include one of the twelve principles of economic thinking and give an example of an application.
   Example: The idea of marginal analysis made the most impression on me. It has helped me think about the relevant costs and benefits of an action. For example, when deciding whether to buy additional products when there is a "buy one get one half off" promotion, I consider whether the second one is worth the additional price.

2. Full-credit answers should include one of the four modules and give an example of an application.
   Example: The module on public choice economics was the most interesting to me. It helped me understand why many people choose not to be informed about politics, and sometimes don't even vote at all.

